LIFE IN WARTIME BRITAIN

Life in
WARTIME
BRITAIN

E. R. CHAMBERLIN

English Life Series
EDITED BY PETER QUENNELL

LONDON: B. T. Batsford Ltd

First published 1972

© E. R. Chamberlin 1972

ISBN 0 7134 1464 2

Filmset by Keyspools Ltd, Golborne, Lancs.
Made and printed in Great Britain
for the publishers
B. T. BATSFORD LTD
4 Fitzhardinge Street, London W1

Contents

The Illustrations

The author and publishers wish to thank the following for permission to reproduce the illustrations listed below: The *Daily Mirror* and Syndication International for fig. 95; Fox Photos Ltd. for figs. 48, 49, 54; The Imperial War Museum for fig. 38; The National Film Archive for figs. 96 and 97; The Radio Times Hulton Picture Library for figs. 1–37, 39–47, 50–3, 55–94, 98–103.

I

Gear-change

On 11 March 1939 *Picture Post* reported that a Mr Albert Smith had been able to buy a set of false teeth for which he paid £3 9s 9d. Mr Smith had been toothless for three years for he had been without a job for three years: as a result of publicity in the magazine he had at last been offered work—digging air-raid shelters in Southwark.

On 13 April 1939 the Ministry of Health issued, without a great deal of publicity, a total of 1,000,000 burial forms to local authorities. Over the following months the local authorities, with equal discretion, began to stockpile coffins. They were made either of papier mâché or stout cardboard, collapsible for ease of stowing: timber was out of the question for it was calculated that in the first three months of a modern war the traditional means of burial would require some 60,000,000 square feet of coffin timber at a cost of nearly £1 million.

Mr Smith's good fortune, and the blizzard of official forms, were the result of a nightmare calculation that had been taking place over the past twenty years. Popular imagination and official projection were, for once, in harmony: 'war' and 'Armageddon' were now virtually synonymous terms. The cinema had helped to thrust that message home to those who could not or would not read: the film version of the immensely popular *Things To Come* had spelt out, in Gothic detail, what the invention of aircraft could—and therefore would—do to civilisation. For twenty years the public had thrilled to the exploits of intrepid aviators, applauding them as they flipped dizzily between continents, passing with contemptuous ease over oceans and deserts, forests, mountains—and cities. But behind the goggled, smiling, waving young man or woman, the least imaginative person could discern, clearly enough, the figure of Apollyon on his great wings. 'The bomber will always get through,' Stanley Baldwin enunciated with, it seems, a certain relish and the people believed this, at least.

And while the newspapers organised their stunts and Amy Johnson became a national heroine and the Schneider Trophy race was followed by millions who had never seen an aeroplane, quiet men with slide rules and statistics etched in a portrait of Apollyon himself. They changed it from time to time, adding a detail here, deleting one there, but the changes were to make him ever more horrific.

Bombing experience in the first World War provided the first rough outlines of the portrait. The outlines were very rough because the experience was very limited. The overwhelming proportion of deaths in that war had been achieved in the traditional manner—by projecting an object between two persons, both of whom were standing or floating on the surface of the planet. Out of the millions killed in that manner, only 1,413 had been killed, in Great Britain, by dropping an object from a great height. But the newly formed Air Ministry had to start somewhere and it took, as point of departure, the eighteen air raids which the Germans had launched over Britain in the last year of the war. An estimated 300 tons of bombs were dropped, causing 4,820 casualties—an acceptable sixteen casualties for every ton dropped over the country as a whole.

But an enemy air force would not waste its strength on villages and country towns. Its natural prey would be the great cities of the kingdom—London, above all—and here it was found that the total casualties per ton of bombs ranged between fifty-two and 121, depending upon whether the raid took place in the daytime, when people were concentrated in shops and offices and factories, or at night-time when they were dispersed in their homes. Balancing all the factors, the Air Ministry came to the conclusion that it would be reasonable to expect an average of fifty casualties per ton in urban areas, one-third of which would be fatal.

That was in the early 1920s. Over the next decade the figure was adjusted fractionally on purely theoretical grounds. Then,

Corporation employees painting kerbstones in Leicester before first national blackout trial, January 1938

in 1936, came the great dress rehearsal of the Spanish Civil War and the figure began to move steadily upwards. In March 1938 the bombing of Barcelona provided a new, apparently absolute and certainly horrifying base-figure: forty-two tons of bombs created 3,000 casualties—a ratio of seventy-two per ton.

Parallel with the soaring estimates of casualties per ton were the equally soaring estimates of the tonnage likely to be dropped on the outbreak of war. The total weight of bombs dropped on London during the heaviest raid of the war had been a mere three tons. In 1922 the Committee of Imperial Defence judged it likely that a 'continental enemy' could drop seventy-five tons each day for an indefinite period. A little over a decade later the theoretical 'continental enemy' had a name and identity and, observing the astonishing progress of the Luftwaffe, the Air Ministry came to the conclusion that a mass attack on London could result in 3,500 tons of bombs in the first twenty-four hours, with a daily average thereafter of 700 tons for an indefinite period. Equating these figures with the numbers of casualties per ton, the Air Ministry came to the conclusion that the civil authorities would do well to assume that there would be 600,000 dead and 1,200,000 injured in the first sixty days of war. The printing order for a million burial forms was put in hand.

At about the time that Albert Smith was drawing his first week's pay, Sir John Anderson was robustly defining the purposes of the organisation which he headed and which was giving work to thousands of unemployed. Personally, he disliked the term 'Air Raid Precautions', preferring the term 'Civil Defence' as one which not only had a wider but a more positive meaning. The object of ARP was not to make everybody safe but 'to make possible an efficient resistance to an aggressor. People expect others—soldiers, sailors, airmen—to take ghastly risks in their service and then say: "We expect absolute safety for ourselves." This is fantastic.' With this bracing reminder that the looming war was to be truly democratic the British people set about preparing what defence they could against the winged terror. The primary impulse was atavistic—to crawl into a hole and hide. On Monday, 26 September 1938, office workers taking the air in Hyde Park had something new to look at, the ugly new gashes of trenches which were beginning to score the turf. Similar trenches were being dug in scores of other open spaces which only a week before had borne notices 'Keep Off the Grass'. All over the country householders were descending reluctantly into musty cellars, wondering where to put the coal and whether pneumonia was really preferable to high explosive. On the Friday evening Neville Chamberlain returned triumphantly, waving his piece of paper, and the bulk of the population thankfully turned their backs on the problem. But

Digging ARP shelters in miniature golf course, Lincoln Inn Fields: September 27, 1938

Peace in our time: Neville Chamberlain at Heston Airport: September 30, 1938

Anderson shelters arrive in Islington: February 1939

the sudden, terrifying apparition of war had drawn the attention of officialdom to a hitherto unimportant fact: tens of thousands of houses had no cellars and those which did were likely to prove death-traps. In the November of 1938 Anderson launched the project which was to make his name one of the household words of the war. The Anderson shelter came into being.

The shelter was simply a shell of corrugated steel, six feet high, four and a half feet wide and six and a half feet long, designed to support earth. It was buried to a depth of four feet and at least fifteen inches of soil had to be heaped over its curved roof. Those who were fortunate enough to have their shelters built on sloping ground could gain access to it relatively comfortably: others had to slither down a kind of trench to reach the low entry. Inside, there was nothing—just the cold, steel shell and its unpleasant association with a tomb. Whatever its potentiality as a shelter, its most obvious characteristic was that of a well, for water seeped in continually—a defect that could be overcome only by frequent bailing or pumping.

The Anderson shelter was issued free to all those with an income below £250 a year, and at a charge of £7 for all those above: altogether, some 2¼ million of them were erected. During the last, uneasy months of peace they appear to have been universally disliked. The public has little confidence in them, the *Nineteenth Century* reported in its issue for September

1939: '"Wouldn't get me in one of those things," said one shopkeeper. "Proper death traps they are in my opinion. A pal of mine over Islington way has turned his upside down and filled it with water for a duckpond—and that's about the best thing you can do with them."' But the man in Islington was not typical: most people might dislike them but obediently erected them and in the first autumn of the war Mass Observation was able to report that 'most people have taken considerable trouble over making their shelters as comfortable and safe as possible'. The exteriors were made gay with wallflowers and nasturtiums and, in time, official and private ingenuity transformed the interiors, notably by adapting the supports to make four bunks. Nevertheless, the universal opinion was that only dire necessity would bring them into use.

The issue of Andersons touched only a proportion of the population, some twenty-seven per cent in all using them as shelters: the issue of gas masks touched every human being in the islands from the very old to the very young, including those who lived at the centre of the great conurbations and those in the remotest farm houses. Mass Observation, indeed, was of the opinion that gas-mask carrying was one of the great unifying factors at the beginning of the war and deplored its decline as the loss of an important outward symbol of national unity.

The fear of gas dominated all other fears, for it arose from no vague Wellsian vision of Armageddon but from actual memory of its terrifying use on the Western Front. Tens of thousands of citizens had had personal experience of it, either directly—

watching their comrades die in agony—or indirectly through those who had been blinded or, perhaps worse, maimed and were now wasting away years after the war ended. The very first circular which the Air Raid Precautions Department put out on its foundation in 1935 dealt predominantly with anti-gas measures. ARP workers were introduced to that strange, subjective list of odours—'musty hay, geranium, peardrops'—which stood in for the gases themselves: later, they cautiously sniffed tiny phials of the lethal stuff and so gained the nearest first-hand knowledge possible.

By January 1937 'civilian-type respirators' were being produced at the rate of 150,000 a week: by the time of the Munich Crisis of September 1938, thirty-eight million had been issued. The distribution of the masks introduced the population as a whole to that social cooperation which was to be a characteristic of the coming six years. In homes throughout the country, where strangers never entered from one year's end to the next, there descended an army of volunteers, the public-spirited minority who had learned a vital craft and were now passing it on to the once-indifferent majority. The fitting of the mask was simplicity itself—it had been designed so that, literally, a child could put it on—but fears had to be overcome and warnings given. The heavy make-up favoured by women at the time was apt to be a liability: temperature rose inside the mask and mascara, in particular, was likely to run. Elaborate hairstyles reduced the protection afforded, for the mask had to fit absolutely snug: when war actually broke out there was a heavy run on hair-dressers for a few weeks and shingled hair came back briefly. Heavily-bearded men were faced with a similar problem and choice. Condensation was likely to build up on the face-piece. Enterprising manufacturers promptly put out patent compounds to overcome the defect but most people found that soap and water or, in an emergency—when the masks were most likely to be required—common spit, did the job as well if not better.

The majority of children took to the masks with little trouble and for the very young was the imaginative 'Mickey Mouse' mask to give grim necessity the appearance of a game. But mothers of babies in arms were faced with a peculiar and personal nightmare. The baby was placed bodily in what was termed a gas helmet but was, in fact, a miniature air-tight chamber into which filtered air was pumped by means of a hand bellows. It needed little imagination to realise what would happen to the child if the person pumping were to be incapacitated, and there was no one to take over.

On 15 March 1939 Czechoslovakia paid the price of the Munich deal and began to break up: on the 15th Adolph Hitler ritually installed himself in the Hradcany Palace in Prague: on the 31st the British Prime Minister personally assured the Poles that the French and British would hasten to their assistance if attacked. It was a gesture and he knew it to be a gesture, no more. 'He says that the futility of it all is the thing that is frightful,' the American ambassador recorded. 'After all, they cannot save the Poles.'

Slowly, with infinite reluctance, the British people advanced to war. On 26 April the first peace-time conscription in the history of the country was announced, but in terms so lacklustre as to throw grave doubts on its purpose. 'Some measure of compulsory military training has, for the time being, become necessary,' Chamberlain informed the House in the tones of a man keeping one foot firmly on the bottom. In July the first Minister of Supply was appointed, theoretically as the co-ordinator of the country's war economy, in practice with powers that allowed him to be little more than the quarter-master of the three Services.

On 11 August the Home Office staged a grand preview of the war with a trial blackout in London. Thousands of people surged into the West End as though the event had been planned for their special entertainment. Alex Glendenning was standing in Piccadilly Circus, gathering impressions for the *Nineteenth Century Review*. 'What I hoped for was a sudden inky plunge as the clock-hand touched the half-hour (12.30 a.m.) but the authorities were not concerned for dramatic effect and the darkness came gradually. Leicester Square and Shaftesbury Avenue were already doused and here and there a lamp went off in Piccadilly until only the big triple-headed lamps in the Circus itself remained alight. Just before they went out I was moved off the island by a policeman and when the final plunge came and the crowd went Ooooh! I was standing among the bonnets of taxicabs and missed the drama.' Fights broke out

Preparing for blackout in London, January 1938   *Sunday, September 3rd, 1939*

everywhere almost immediately—'one recalled vaguely that sandbags were once used for other purposes than ARP'. Others noticed the mixture of hilarity and near-hysteria as pedestrians blundered into each other and into sandbagged obstructions. Glendenning came to the conclusion that the test was a fiasco, largely due to the glaring headlights of vehicles which provided 'an illuminated diagram of our main thoroughfare'. Officialdom came to the same conclusion, with results that were to cost hundreds of lives.

At 4.45 a.m. on 1 September the German army crossed the Polish frontier. At 9 a.m. on Sunday, 3 September the British ultimatum that the troops be withdrawn was handed to an embarrassed official of the German government. He did not seem to know what to do with it but it was, in any case, a formality. It expired, unanswered, at 11 a.m. 'Britain was the first country in the world to go to war with Hitler's Germany without first being attacked herself,' the Ministry of Information boasted but it was only a marginal distinction for the French declaration followed at 5 p.m. Australia and New Zealand declared war without consulting their parliaments: for the second time in a generation the sub-continent of India found itself, with the Colonies, willy-nilly, involved in an incomprehensible war between Europeans: South Africa hesitated but under the prodding of Jan Christian Smuts came in on 6 September and Canada followed on the 10th. The British Empire, for the last time in its history, was acting as an entity.

On 28 September 1938 thirty-four per cent of the British population believed that war was imminent. On 31 August 1939—twelve hours before the German tanks rolled into Poland and seventy-two hours before the British ultimatum was delivered—the proportion had sunk to eighteen per cent. Among the optimistic eighty-two per cent were those wealthy enough or enterprising enough to take their summer holiday on the Continent. Spread out from Athens to Helsinki, from Pompeii to Reykjavik, they stopped in their tracks to race home before the drawbridge was raised, clutching their thick, dignified blue passports with their exhortation to all foreigners to aid and cherish these subjects of His Britannic Majesty. Some found the passport an embarrassment, the badge of an island people again withdrawing themselves from the contagion of the Continent. Some found them a godsend. Few found them of much use with their own officials. In Cannes, Brian Howard found that 'All that was left of HM Government, of King Edward VII and Lord Brougham was the following frosty notice pinned to a locked and empty consulate:

> British subjects enquiring about the political situation should be told that the Consulates have no more information than appears in the Press and the Wireless. . . . British subjects when asking about their present situation should be told that the responsibility for their plans rests on their own shoulders and not on the shoulders of their consular offices in this connection.'

Most made it back to the Channel ports. There, in the thronged customs sheds and on the overcrowded ferries, there was excitement and confusion but little hysteria, little selfishness. There was, perhaps, the titled lady who tried to thrust her way forward, demanding of a steward 'Don't you know who I am?' His vigorous reply—'I know you're a bitch. Take your place in the queue'—was probably the first recorded version of that 'Don't you know there's a war on,' which was to become a national slogan. But the titled lady survived into folklore largely because of her rarity.

Passing the stream of homecoming exiles was another, smaller stream—Continental citizens leaving the island kingdom to its own devices. Among them was a young man of twenty-three, wearing a remarkably scruffy mackintosh—William Joyce, bound for several weeks of uncertainty and humiliation in Berlin and, thereafter, fame of a kind.

Those who returned on the afternoon of the first day of war found that Apollyon had already spread his shadow over Britain—or at least so their friends believed and insisted. At about the time that Neville Chamberlain was broadcasting to the people, telling them that, for the second time in a generation, they were at war with the Germans, a French aircraft crossed the Channel unheralded. At 11.28 a.m. over most of England people heard, for the first time under war conditions, that eerie rising and falling note of the sirens which the Home

Taking shelter: September 1939

Air raid shelter for sentry   *A short-lived attempt to beat the blackout*

Office poetically described as 'warbling'. It was precisely what was expected, the first delivery of the expected 3,500 tons of bombs within half an hour of declaration of war. The fact that no one actually heard a bomb or saw an enemy aircraft merely proved that the attack had taken place elsewhere and 'They' were keeping quiet about it.

But if any felt a sense of anti-climax their forebodings were justified as night fell: for the first time in the history of civilisation total darkness wrapped the cities. The blackout, which endured from 1 September 1939 to 17 September 1944, was perhaps the most hated of all emergency regulations. Nevertheless, dreary symbol of war though it was in its negativeness, its all-pervasiveness, paradoxically the population clung to it, fiercely defending it from transgressors. The regulations had official teeth and throughout the war careless citizens trooped through the police courts, listened to indignant homilies from the bench, and paid their fines. But the common citizen was the most effective watchdog, particularly in the first months of war. It became a social solecism to allow a chink of light to penetrate and the recalcitrant were likely to have stones hurled through their windows. The widespread instinct to defend the blackout arose from a simple, atavistic reaction: if the enemy could not see you he could not hurt you. During that first September the regulations imposed a total absence of light: fanatics claimed that even a white, upturned face or a glowing cigarette could provide a target. There was a ban on torches and, far more seriously, on car headlights. Crossing a city street after dark was, quite literally, a game of chance and during that month casualties from road accidents rose by 100 per cent. After the first panic reaction with its appalling results the regulations were eased. Car headlights were permitted with the use of masks which threw a narrow beam directly downwards; torches, heavily shrouded or masked were also permitted, creating thereby one of the great treasure-hunts of the war—the search for the 'No 8' battery which would fit a small pocket torch. Curbs and steps were daubed with white paint: masked illuminated signs advertised that such and such a pub or shop was OPEN.

But nothing could relieve the tedium, the dreary duty of 'doing the blackouts', the domestic chore that was performed nearly 2,000 times within half an hour of sunset. Most people eventually adopted one of two systems, either shutters or curtains. Shutters were heavy to lift and cumbersome to insert, but they could be made of any opaque material. Curtains required precious fabric. The government had laid in large stocks of the funereal stuff at the beginning of the war but inevitably supplies ran out and there was the constant need to repair the ravages of use. Blackout material joined the other materials in short supply, soaring in price. In desperation householders used ordinary fabrics, making them opaque with an officially recommended 'blackout mixture', a viscous compound of size and lampblack. The blackout in factories tended to be a permanent feature: factories with large expanses of skylights and windows found it impossible to devise moveable screens and the glass was simply painted over, condemning the workers to artificial light day and night throughout the war.

'If those Germans think they can frighten me by sitting up in those balloons all the time, they're very much mistaken,' a 'dear old lady' was supposed to have remarked on first seeing a barrage balloon in flight. Apochryphal or not, she was certainly atypical, for most people regarded the portly silver monsters with actual affection. They were first seen, over London, on 9 October 1938 but thereafter they floated over every city that was likely to be an enemy target, now dispersed, now concentrated according to the ebb and flow of the air war.

At first it was assumed that they were positive in action, one of the endless 'secret weapons' of the war: some believed that the cables were magnetised to attract either bombs or aircraft, others claimed that the balloons were filled with explosive gases or that anti-aircraft guns were to be suspended from them. But even when their true role was known confidence did not decline, for it was felt that they placed one more obstacle between the falling bomb and cringing human flesh. Official propaganda went to considerable lengths to support the belief: the Ministry of Information film, *The Lion Has Wings*, contained a preposterous sequence in which a German air fleet was seen recoiling in abject terror from the balloon barrage of London. In military terms their purpose was strictly limited, nothing more than deterring low-level raiders, in particular the Stuka dive-bomber which had acquired such a terrifying reputation on the Continent, but their cost was probably justified in terms of morale alone. Curiously, no popular generic term was coined for them, as 'Moaning Minnie' was coined for the warning siren: they had, perhaps, too many subjective shapes—whales, sausages, elephants, fish, boxing gloves—for any one to impress itself on the popular imagination.

Groping through the blackout, clutching their gas masks, burrowing into the earth: banned from all places of public

Barrage balloon exercise: October 1938

entertainment, registered and documented: exhorted, congratulated and threatened by an ever-increasing flood of official propaganda, the people awaited the opening of the gates of hell. The gates which opened, however, gave entry to what more closely resembled a bureaucratic waiting room. There was no excitement to compensate for deprivations, no great patriotic upsurge as there had been in the first weeks of the war still known as Great. The climate had drastically changed in twenty years. It was no longer possible to stir patriotic blood by large references to King and Country: the Oxford Union resolution in February 1933 had made that very clear. But neither did the anaemic intellectual call to make the world safe from Fascism have much impact. The handful of people who had been aware of the true nature of the regimes in Germany and Italy were either linked, in the popular mind, with the spectre of Bolshevism, or belonged to the derided class of 'intellectuals'. The domestic achievements of the regimes had been admired, even envied—'Mussolini made the trains run to time: Hitler cut unemployment'—while the foreign adventures had, so far, not touched the British directly.

In compensation for the lack of patriotism was the lack of the puerile xenophobia which, in the previous war, had found expression in the kicking of dachshunds and the banning of Beethoven. Even at the height of the war, when millions had experienced the agonies and the terrors of the Blitz, George Orwell could tell the Americans: 'Hun has not caught on with the working classes this time. They call Germans "Jerries" which may have a mildly obscene meaning but is not unfriendly. The Italians are generally called Eyeties, which is less offensive than Wops and there is no popular feeling against them whatever. As to the smaller nations who are supposed to be at war with us, no one remembers which is which.' Despite the pressures, the popular mind insisted on making a distinction between 'Nazi' and 'German'. When the *Graf Spee* was cornered in Montevideo harbour in December 1939, popular sympathy for the trapped crew followed swiftly on the pride felt in the exploit. Harold Nicolson recorded in his diary: 'I loathe the idea of these brave men steaming out in cold blood either to our destruction or their destruction. We simply do not want either side to win in this combat. There will be no sense of triumph or defeat whatever happens to the Spee.' Its captain, Langdorf, became a tragic figure when he scuttled his ship, on Hitler's orders, and then committed suicide. A housewife in Tyneside broke down when asked for her reactions: 'Oh, I could weep, I feel I have lost a friend. Another brave man gone and Hitler and Co live.' In Ipswich a factory worker remarked: 'He was a good chap. Treated his prisoners well. It shows there are some decent men in the German navy.' A newspaper cartoon showed him as a handsome, idealised victim of Nazism.

At home, the skies remained innocent of bombers: abroad, the great armies of the warring nations lay in the 'sinister trance' of Churchill's phrase. Denied the stimulation of hatred, or patriotism, or fear the people sank into a profound apathy.

The controversial poster: who was 'Us'?

The gap between leaders and the led widened. YOUR COURAGE: YOUR CHEERFULNESS: YOUR RESOLUTION WILL BRING US VICTORY the strident posters proclaimed but the cynical merely noted the distinction between 'You' and 'Us'. Kingsley Wood, Secretary for Air, contributed his mite to wartime anecdotage when asked to set fire to the Black Forest. 'Are you aware it is private property? Why, you will be asking me to bomb Essen next.' The Prime Minister applauded the patriotic series of lunches organised at the Dorchester during November. 'They will, I am sure, have a steadying affect on morale on the Home Front which will be most valuable.'

Later, he unwisely descended into the demotic. 'Hitler has missed the bus,' he proclaimed as the trance grew deeper.

Promptly, Hitler caught the bus: the British Expeditionary Force withdrew from Norway, beginning that series of retreats which earned for its initials BEF the flippant Back Every Friday. Undismayed, the Prime Minister essayed a flight of rhetoric. 'Today our wings are spread over the Arctic. They are sheathed in ice. Tomorrow the sun of victory will touch them with its golden light.' Parliament stirred.

The Phoney War, the Sitzkrieg, the Great Bore War ended, for Britain, shortly before nine o'clock on the evening of 7 May 1940. At precisely 3.48 that afternoon Neville Chamberlain had risen to address the House, explaining and defending the débâcle in Norway. Four and a half hours later his friend and colleague, Leo Amery, brought a passionate debate to an end, arising in his turn to make the Cromwellian thrust. 'You have sat here too long for any good that you have been doing. Depart I say, and let us have done with you. In the name of God, go!' The debate spilled over into the following day, but the work of surgery was done. It had taken the Commons a little over ninety minutes to destroy an honourable old man whose greatest error had been to assume that another man who had given his word intended to keep it. It had taken the country, as a whole, eight months and four days of supposedly total war to effect a change of gear. Three days later Winston Churchill 'acquired the chief power in the state which henceforth I wielded in ever growing measure for five years and three months of total war'. But on that same day of 10 May on which the new Prime Minister received his seals of office the German army erupted across the frontiers of the German state. Six weeks later the war in the West was virtually over.

Neville Chamberlain died of cancer in October 1940: a year later George Orwell wrote his epitaph. 'His opponents professed to see in him a dark and wily schemer plotting to sell England to Hitler, but it is far likelier that he was merely a stupid old man doing his best according to his very dim lights. Like the mass of people he did not want to pay the price of either peace or war.' The epitaph was rendered cruel as much by memory of recent danger as by political difference but it embodied an essential truth. During at least two-and-a-half years of his three-year premiership, Neville Chamberlain more accurately reflected the inchoate desires of the British people than did the pugnacious Winston Churchill or those, such as Orwell himself, calling their warning from the opposite end of the political spectrum. The commercial song-writers, ever alert to popular trends, gave the Man with the Umbrella their dingy accolade in the first few weeks of war:

> *God Bless you, Mr Chamberlain,*
> *We're all mighty proud of You.*
> *You look swell holding your umbrella,*
> *All the world loves a wonderful feller—so*
> *God bless you Mr Chamberlain.*

'Like the mass of people he did not want to pay the price of peace or war.'

Further Reading
T. H. O'Brien, *Civil Defence** (1955), gives the official account of ARP; Mass Observation, *War Begins at Home* (1940), gives the citizen's view. For events leading up to the outbreak see Taylor, *English History*; estimates of potential aerial attack in R. M. Titmuss, *Problems of social policy** (1950), Chapter 1. Chapter 15 of Ronald Blythe's *Age of Illusion* gives a vivid account of Chamberlain's fall.

II

The Citizen Army

Punch, as ever, had a word for it. On 22 May 1940 it published Bernard Partridge's cartoon in which John Bull, interrupted in his gardening by an enemy airfleet passing overhead, reaches for a rifle propped up against the shed door. Cartoonists embroidered the theme again and again during that summer, their contributions ranging from Low's stark 'Very well—alone!' uttered by a defiant soldier on the cliffs of Dover to Osbert Lancaster's irritated clubman 'Waiter, just go and ask those fellows if they're members here'—the 'fellows' being enemy soldiers armed to the teeth. Pride in imperturbability struggled with a schoolboy sense of excitement. From Wolverhampton the *Daily Mail* racing correspondent filed a report that would have done justice to Sir Francis Drake. 'The people were stunned by the news [of the fall of France] just after the first race at Wolverhampton yesterday but, of course, carried on and presumably the meeting today will go through, if only as a gesture of stoutness.'

The patriotism which, a year before, had seemed as dead as the Divine Right now flourished as a primitive, vigorous tribalism under the stimulus of a wholly new threat. Britain was about to be invaded. Looking back on those highly charged weeks between June and September, between the fall of France and the Battle of Britain, Margery Allingham noted that they differed, qualitatively, not only from the period before but also the period after, forming an epoch in themselves. 'There was more than a touch of the address before Agincourt in the air, a secret satisfaction that if it was coming we were to be the chosen. All this looks childish if written down but it was a direct, childish time, quite different from but more entirely satisfying than any other piece of life which I at least have encountered.' Immediately contemporary diarists and correspondents substantiated the hindsight. The diaries of the period, whatever the skill of the writer, show a qualitative change—a tautening, a laconism. There was fear of the unknown, but there was also a sense of excitement, and a wholly irrational sense of relief that the British people were now responsible for their own survival, unencumbered by allies.

As late as 17 September Churchill warned the House, in a secret session, that the enemy might try to land half-a-million men. It was assumed that the Luftwaffe had some 6,000 aircraft—bombers and fighters—with which to launch the long-delayed paralysing blow, although, in fact, there were less than 3,000 German aircraft on the entire Western Front. But it was neither the ancient fear of sea invasion, nor the modern fear of mass-bombing which predominated in the first few weeks. Both were there, but as a general, background fear. In the foreground there loomed a figure taken from a childish nightmare, the bogeyman who could appear anywhere, at anytime, irresistibly —the paratrooper. The bogeyman was the product of the brilliant use made of parachute troops during the conquest of the Low Countries. Forming an entirely new arm, their limitations had yet to be exposed, and both popular and official imagination endowed them with almost superhuman qualities. The Air Ministry sent out a warning that 'German parachute

AA gun site in Hyde Park

troops, when descending, hold their arms above their heads as if surrendering. The parachutist, however, holds a grenade in each hand.' The paratrooper would, indeed, have had to have been a legendary figure if he could control his parachute, land, and disentangle himself while clutching two live grenades, but the warning was of a piece with the rumours that swept across the Channel in the wake of the defeated armies. The most extraordinary of these was the paratrooper's almost protean ability to disguise himself in some innocuous form—usually as nursemaid, parson, or nun. The pure fantasy of the idea of a burly male in his twenties, cramming himself into a nun's habit in order to float down on a land where nuns were a rarity was index enough to the hysteria that lay not far from the excitement and resolution.

Side by side with the figure of the parachutist—and, indeed, combining with it—was the sinister figure of the Fifth Columnist. The phrase was one of Spain's many legacies to modern war. In 1936 one of General Franco's commanders announced that he had five columns attacking Madrid, four advancing upon it in battle order and the fifth—composed of sympathisers —operating in the capital itself. The Fifth Columnist was even more protean than the paratrooper, for he reflected the nation's own uncertainty as to its collective will to resist. Significantly, while spy stories were retold with gusto and imaginative elaboration throughout the war, the Fifth Column scare died out as the nation achieved confidence in its purpose. But in 1940 the Fifth Column was still seen as a positive weapon of war, one to be combated by positive means: in June an emergency regulation prescribed imprisonment or fine for any person convicted of circulating 'any report or statement relating to matters connected with the war which is likely to cause alarm and despondency'. At that period almost any honest statement regarding the war could not be other than pessimistic, 'likely to cause alarm and despondency,' and the provisions of the order were unpleasantly wide, sweeping into the same net the gossip, the honest pessimist and the anti-bureaucrat along with the actively treacherous. Despite the wholesale internment of aliens—hostile and friendly alike—which had taken place at the beginning of the war there were still large numbers of people speaking with heavy foreign accents at large in the country.

If they strayed too far from familiar surroundings they were likely to find themselves surrounded by a hostile crowd. In Manchester, the Spanish-born widow of an Englishman was hailed before the magistrates because she had 'visited air-raid shelters, where her foreign accent alarmed people'. She was discharged, with advice that she must have found difficult to follow: 'If you have to go into a shelter, remember not to make people afraid. You have rather a foreign accent and people are nervous.' Although hindsight makes it seem unlikely that an enemy would have employed agents speaking with heavy foreign accents, popular imagination was accurate enough in this matter. The handful of spies who did, in fact, struggle ashore, were equipped and trained with ludicrous incompetency. One man actually attempted to get a drink in an English pub at nine o'clock in the morning. Ignorance of the remarkable British licensing laws was, perhaps, understandable, but the possession of Continental clothes and food—even, in one case, part of a German sausage—and bulky wireless transmitters in conspicuous suitcases is almost wholly inexplicable. The British opinion of German abilities seems to have been exactly matched by German ignorance of British customs. Shortly before the Nuremberg trials Joachim von Ribbentrop, one-time London socialite, addressed an appeal to a certain Vincent Churchill.

The anti-rumour order issued in June was one of the products of the sweeping Emergency Powers (Defence) Act of 22 May. Passed in a single day, instantaneously it turned the United Kingdom into a military camp whose sole objective was military survival. Civil rights gained over a millenium of bitter struggle were suspended 'for the duration', for the Act thereafter allowed the government to issue, without further recourse to Parliament, what orders and regulations it considered necessary to prosecute the war. A libertarian's nightmare, it was a bureaucrat's paradise and, faithfully, the orders poured out: 2,000 of them were issued within twelve months of the passing of the Act, each of them affecting the citizen in areas hitherto untouched by legislation. He could be ordered to leave his home or stay in it: if he possessed a farm or even a smallholding he could be told what crops to plant, where and, on certain ludicrous occasions when bureaucratic zeal outran agricultural knowledge, when to plant them. His clothes, his journeys, his food, his entertainment all were now subject to control. The community began to learn how to balance itself on the knife-edge between the demands of defence in total war and the naked operations of a police state. The proposal to set up Zone courts in areas in which 'by reason of recent or immediately apprehended enemy action' the normal courts could not operate seemed, on the surface, an eminently sensible precaution—the creation of a breakwater against anarchy. But Parliament disliked the sweeping powers of the projected courts—in particular the powers to pass death sentences—and the thin edge of that potential wedge was blunted by the provision that such sentences would be subject to review.

The first wave of orders were produced by the imminent threat of invasion but long after that threat had receded into the background the orders remained in force. The order which created the greatest confusion for the citizen, with the least inconvenience to the enemy, was that which decreed the obliteration of all signs which could identify a locality. It came into force in May 1940 and, though subsequently modified, remained in force until six months before the end of the war. It was undoubtedly the almost wholly imaginary threat of the ubiquitous parachutist which led to the order. Even the most optimistic of official minds could hardly have envisaged an invading army losing its way in the gentle countryside of southern England because of the lack of signposts. But it might have discomfited the odd parachutist descending from heaven into a hostile world.

It certainly discomfited hundreds of citizens going about their lawful occasions. With rigorous logic the order decreed that not only should the traveller not be shown the way to a place but also that he should not know that he was there when he had arrived. In addition to the uprooting of signposts and milestones—some of them centuries old—place names in towns and villages were obliterated. It was only when the immense operation was actually undertaken that it was appreciated how strong was the human instinct for identification. Churches proclaimed their local allegiance together with branches of national concerns—banks, shops, building societies: it was argued that a determined parachutist could force his way into any of these branches and find stacks of headed notepaper, each

The travellers' nightmare: uprooted signposts

sheet bearing the name of the locality. In some areas buses and trams lost their destination boards; elsewhere street names derived from neighbouring localities were swept away and for more than two years innumerable 'London Roads, Brighton Roads, Liverpool Roads' and the like were wrapped in anonymity. Railway stations were allowed to display signs, but under such complex regulations concerning size and visibility as to make them all but useless to the traveller. The lack of name-plates in towns was little more than an irritation even if it seemed the most pointless of regulations: writers-to-the Press had a field day pointing out that it was hardly possible to conceal the identity of Canterbury or York from any reasonably cultured enemy soldier. But the lack of rural signposts was immensely inconvenient and, at times, dangerous. More than one traveller, reluctant to ask his way for fear of being taken for a spy, blundered into a 'Forbidden Zone', with its risk of a trigger-happy sentry shooting first and explaining afterwards.

The blotting out of identities was succeeded, on 13 June, by the banning of church bells. Thereafter, they would be sounded only as warning of parachutists. Arbitrary edict brought popular protest. The legitimate objection was made that such an act automatically made every church in the land a military target. It was, in any case, a short-sighted provision. Admittedly, the church bell was the obvious means of making a loud signal in all communities, remote as well as urban, but the church was the only class of public building which was not on the telephone—and presumably speed was desirable in passing

32

the warning message from headquarters to the church. Campanologists also pointed out, with a certain grim relish, that an inexperienced bell-ringer ran a good chance of breaking his neck. Authority remained unmoved and the sound which, for centuries, had been associated with joy and tranquillity now became charged with high menace.

The fear of invasion produced a remarkable crop of rubbish heaps across acres of open countryside. Every piece of flat ground which could reasonably—or fancifully—accommodate a landing aircraft was strewn with obstacles—old cars, goal posts, prams, treetrunks. Bitter arguments arose between the custodians of cricket pitches and sporting fields and even bowling greens and the more fanatical defenders of the island kingdom who were cavalierly proposing to deface the sacred turf. These temporary obstacles could be, eventually, removed: a permanent garnish to the landscape was given by the hundreds of 'pill-boxes' and tank-traps—lines of concrete 'teeth'—erected in a few frenetic weeks. The tank-traps were erected on or near major roads and postwar land-hunger ensured that most of these, too, would be demolished in time: a large number of 'pill-boxes' were constructed in the depths of the country and form the last tangible monument of the era. Squat, massive structures, designed to act as strong-points, their demolition would have cost more than their site was worth and they remain to puzzle future archaeologists—or even contemporary military strategists for their siting is frequently bizarre.

It was on the evening of 14 May—only a few hours after the Dutch Army had surrendered—that there occurred the final eccentric flowering of the citizen militia in the United Kingdom. On that evening Anthony Eden, Secretary of State for War, broadcast an appeal for all men between the ages of seventeen and sixty-five to enrol themselves in an organisation to be known as the Local Defence Volunteers. Their primary purpose was to deal with the threat of the parachutist: their sole medical qualification was to be 'capable of free movement'; preferably, they should have some experience of arms but this was not decreed as essential—a fact which was to create some hair-raising incidents. The response could not have been more immediate, for even while he was speaking the first volunteers were appearing at their local police station. The police were

Dr Jocelin Perkins, Sacrist of Westminster Abbey, being drilled by a member of Westminster LDV

Member of a woman's section, LDV

sometimes taken by surprise: in one Kentish village, the local policeman encountered what he took to be a mob of armed men and angrily ordered them to give up their arms, for it was illegal for civilians to carry them. In Kent alone 10,000 had volunteered within the first twenty-four hours; within a month the new force numbered nearly a million and a half. In July Churchill referred to it as the 'Home Guard' and the short, vigorous phrase was immediately adopted.

The search for arms predominated during the first few weeks. One volunteer in Sussex remembered: 'We raked over the whole district for firearms. I think a few people were scared by our enquiries as they had overlooked the need for taking out gun permits. We heard that a very patriotic woman in the village had shooting irons so we called to see her. One of the walls of her cottage was decorated with guns of all ages and sizes. She willingly lent us two, but she declined to let us take a natty little revolver. "I'm keeping that myself for the first German who sets foot in this village."'

Rural groups found a natural supply of ordinary shotguns; elsewhere museum curators and antique dealers were put under heavy pressure to disgorge anything that would not

34

actually explode when the trigger was pressed. The first major supply of firearms, however, came from a source 4,000 miles distant when the government of the US sent a consignment of half-a-million twenty-year-old rifles. Gradually, British war production was able to feed the hungry new organisation and ultimately Home Guard equipment differed little from that of the regular army. Ironically, it was reasonably well equipped with conventional weapons when its greatest legend came into being: in 1941 the War Office produced a curious hybrid weapon—a length of steel piping with a bayonet welded on—which it proudly described as a 'pike'. The mockery which greeted the weapon ensured that few were issued but it was to form a fruitful subject for comedians, both then and twenty-five years afterwards.

The Home Guard lasted as a true guerilla force for barely three months: called into being by the threat of invasion in June 1940, it altered its character when the threat receded into the background, becoming rationalised or ossified, depending on the viewpoint. In its heroic period it was not so much democratic as anarchic: no formal ranks were envisaged and there was much heated controversy about the propriety of saluting. Piquant situations were created when the local commander, chosen because of his local knowledge and not his social or military eminence, might find himself giving orders to

Home Guard exercise: the new techniques of war

a full-scale general. Some of the high-ranking officers who came out of retirement to serve insisted on parading in full regimental glory to the embarrassment or amusement of their comrades. The traditional fought a strong rearguard action against the concept of the Home Guard as a flexible, irregular force. George Orwell's company listened to 'a lecture by General —. Dilating on the Home Guard being a static force he said contemptuously and in a marked way that he saw no use in our practising taking cover "crawling on our stomachs etc". Our job, he said, was to die at our posts. Was also great on bayonet practice and hinted that regular army ranks, saluting etc were to be introduced shortly. These wretched old blimps are merely pathetic in themselves and one would feel rather sorry for them if they were not hanging round our necks like millstones.'

Whatever the Home Guard might have done to the enemy they certainly succeeded in making life not merely uncomfortable but dangerous for their friends. The bewildered motorist, trying to find his way in total darkness through a country denuded of every signpost, stood only too good a chance of colliding with some hastily erected road block. Some of them met, in addition, a hail of bullets. Motorcyclists might encounter the hazard of 'an adjustable trip wire made up of fifty yards of five-strand clothes line, a clothes line pulley and a snatch-block and two picket posts as hold fast: cost 4s 11d— most effective.'

In August 1940 the once independent units were affiliated to country regiments and their spontaneity and flexibility declined. 'Some commanders showed more rigidity than appears to be common in the Regular Army itself . . . orthodoxy has curtailed much of the Home Guard's original freedom and its most unfortunate result has been to place a curb on initiative.' The introduction of conscription at the end of 1941 marked the moment of final change and that change was summed up by a short and bitter letter which appeared in *Picture Post* in April 1944: 'My husband has just returned from a compulsory Home Guard parade. This consisted of an address by his battalion commander on "The early history of India from 1513 to 1717".'

Ironically, while almost every other aspect of the war was given high dramatic treatment in the postwar years, the Home Guard, the only truly spontaneous grouping of the people,

The Citizen Army. CD personnel at march-past

became merely the subject of comedy. In 1969 BBC TV launched a programme under the title of *Dad's Army*, chronicling the comic antics of a Home Guard platoon in a small town. Accurately, the series identified and built up the characters as they had been developed in folklore over the preceding quarter of a century—the pompous, incompetent officer; the ineffectual sergeant: the old sweat; the village simpleton; the wide boy dodging more dangerous service. Hindsight had given the final twist to reality. The mock Sunday-morning battles of 1943 and 1944 were commemorated, the lonely night patrols of 1940 were ignored. The crude, home-made or antiquated weapons were remembered with a smile; it was forgotten that their bearers had had every intention of using them against the most efficient mechanised army the world had seen.

The Home Guard had progressed from spontaneity to regimentation, from flexibility to rigidity. The Civil Defence force reversed the process, beginning as an organisation blue-printed in detail and developing flexibility under the pressures of actual war. The General Strike of 1926 had shown what could happen to a country when its major channels of communication and distribution were paralysed and the government of the day had been forced to adopt a degree of regionalisation. Twelve regions were set up for the purpose of Civil Defence—London itself counting as one region. The chain of control ran down from the Regional Headquarters—that for the London Region was established in the Geological Museum

Brewing up at Warden's Post in London

—through the Group Headquarters to the Borough. This was usually established in the town hall, the Civil Defence services thereby being integrated into the existing urban services. In most towns, council staff were seconded, sharing responsibilities with the small number of full-time Civil Defence workers and the large body of volunteers. Below the Borough lay the District and below that, at the bottom of the whole organisation, lay the Warden's Post.

The number of Wardens' Posts varied according to the density of population: in theory, each was supposed to control an area containing 500 people and in London, therefore, there were approximately ten posts per square mile. The post, heavily sandbagged and clearly marked, would be situated in any building which could withstand blast. It would contain a telephone, a map of the district, camp beds, table, tea-making equipment and very little else. The Post was as liable to be bombed as any other building in the area and the ability to improvise a post out of shattered bits and pieces, and perhaps even set it up in the open street was one which became highly developed. A system of runners was organised to overcome the almost inevitable dislocation of the telephone system in an area under bombardment.

The number of wardens varied, depending not so much upon the density of local population as upon the number of streets to be covered. For the warden was the ultimate unit of the vast structure. It was his first, hurried report of an 'incident' which would set the machinery going, bring stretcher parties, fire engines, rescue squads, mobile canteens—all the services necessary to tend the injured, comfort the survivors and dispose of the dead. And he was, usually, a volunteer.

At the beginning of the war the entire Civil Defence forces totalled some one-and-a-half million men and women, 400,000 of whom were full-time workers paid at the rate of £3 per week. Even at the height of the London raids only 16,000 of the city's 200,000 wardens were full-time. During the long period of the 'phoney war'—and even after the period of heavy raids—these full-timers incurred considerable obloquy. In 1939 and the early months of 1940, when unemployment was still at a high level, they were simultaneously envied and despised for their 'cushy jobs'. In 1939 one of Mass-Observation's observers reported a conversation he had had with a woman whose flooded shelter had recently been pumped out by the local wardens. 'Really, it makes me furious to think of these ARP people raking in money like that from two or three jobs while there are thousands not knowing where they're going to get a cup of tea and a currant bun from at Christmas. I think it's shameful.'

Part of the dislike they aroused was the product of the British dislike of the minor official. In 1938 the Home Office had attempted to define the ideal warden. 'An air-raid warden should regard himself, first and foremost, as a member of the public chosen and trained to be a leader of his fellow citizens and, with them and for them, do the right things in an emergency.' Ultimately, he was, indeed to do the right thing in an emergency and earn praises as a hero but until that emergency came, all that the public saw was a personification of the interfering and incompetent State—a man in flimsy blue overalls wearing an incongruous steel helmet, harrying citizens about their blackout, quizzing them about the number of buckets of sand and water in their offices and in general strutting with a little brief authority. Extreme opinions saw him as the local gauleiter; even the more moderate dismissed him as an interfering busybody drawing £3 a week for his trouble. The fact that he was a local man was a priceless asset in an emergency—he knew who was living where and under what condi-

enrol
at any
fire station

Heavy Rescue worker with experimental
breathing apparatus

Auxiliary Fire Service recruiting poster:
September 1938

tions and so could direct the rescue squads swiftly. But it also undermined his position during the dull days of 'peace' and the no less uneventful phoney war. The official mind seems to have been almost as blind to his vital role as the popular mind. The paid warden's wages were below the average—in July 1940 shop assistants were earning more than £3 16s per week, building workers more than £4 4s. They were at the bottom of the list for the issue of uniforms: it was not until mid-1941 that they obtained heavy-duty clothing to at least the standard issued to the Home Guard. Altogether, the air-raid warden stood as testimony to the British belief in muddling through and leaving everything to the volunteer, a curious contrast to the overall structure of the service of which he was an indispensable unit.

The distinction between ordinary civilian services and operations created by wartime conditions tended to shade one into the other: a gas-fitter might perhaps abandon his work on a domestic cooker to deal with a ruptured main a few feet away from an unexploded bomb; electricians, waterworks staff and telephone engineers would play as vital parts in restoring normality to an area as would the members of the formal Civil

Defence Services. Specific emergency services were an amalgam
of full-time workers and volunteers contributing their specialised skills. The Heavy Rescue Service was composed for the
most part of building workers, whose task was to burrow deep
into the pile of rubble that had once been a building, tunnelling
into the heart of a creaking, shifting mass to locate the victims
and bring them, dead or living, to the surface. The Women's
Voluntary Service drew upon that immense pool of largely
middle-class talent which, in peacetime, formed the major
support of charities in the country. Nationally, the WVS
organisation acted as clearing house for the collection and distribution of the millions of domestic items needed to put a
'bombed-out' family on its feet. Locally, they provided immediate assistance for the dazed and temporarily helpless
victims, as well as an impressive proportion of the millions of
gallons of tea on which the British fought their war. Women
also formed the backbone of the Ambulance Service—both as
drivers as well as nurses: the skill and tenacity with which they
navigated their requisitioned vehicles under almost impossible
conditions should have destroyed the myth of the 'woman
driver'.

The fire services were expanded enormously to cope with the
threat of air raids. Ultimately, members of the Auxiliary Fire
Service outnumbered regular firemen by more than ten to one.
The peacetime fire services had been grossly underpaid but the
semi-military discipline had made them into compact bodies
so that they resented and despised the flood of amateur newcomers. The general public, predictably, praised the AFS as
heroes during the Blitz and castigated them as £3-a-week
loafers during periods of calm. The thousands of Auxiliaries
came from all classes and occupations but the AFS nevertheless
had a curiously homogeneous quality: certainly the newcomer
stood a very good chance of rubbing shoulders with a poet or
novelist. Dylan Thomas sneered at the Service as the Boy's Fire
Brigade. Patric Dickinson apostrophised the Fireman Poet:

> You burn with zeal to fight a fire,
> Who never had a fire to fight.
> Save that within, which you aspire
> (In vain?) to set and keep alight.

It may have been that the very nature of the fire service, its opportunity to fight the universal enemy of civilisation, attracted those who were pacifist by intellect and yet felt impelled to take positive action in defence of their country. It is scarcely a coincidence that two of the rare genuine fragments of war literature—Henry Green's novel *Caught* and William Sansom's picture of frozen time in his short story *The Wall* should have been the direct product of experience in the AFS.

In August 1941 Herbert Morrison, the Minister of Home Security, announced the formation of a new organisation—the Fire Guard—and urged his compatriots to enrol. His compatriots remained unmoved. They had, perhaps, been urged in ringing tones just once too often. The name, perhaps, was unfortunately chosen for 'Fire Guard' aroused memories of only a useful but unglamorous piece of domestic furniture. The nation, for whatever reason, saw the 'new' service for what it was—an attempt to glamorise and ginger up a vital but dreary service—firewatching.

The most destructive weapon hurled against Britain during the six years of war was not the explosive bombs and mines of the early period, nor even the gigantic rockets of the last months, but an innocuous looking, greyish cylinder, a little over a foot long and weighing some two pounds—the incendiary bomb. It depended for its effect upon swamping the defence and was dropped in thousands of clusters. During the few seconds after it had struck and ignited it was perfectly simple

The King and Princess Elizabeth operating a stirrup pump

Firewatchers at dusk

for a level-headed person to extinguish it. All that was required was a smothering agent, preferably sand, and a human hand to apply it. It was the bringing of the human hand to the sand which proved the difficulty.

The government had foreseen the problem, but only in part. In September 1940 a compulsory firewatching order was issued —but this applied only to large factories. The tens of thousands of offices and shops in the centres of cities were left unguarded and the result was spelled out with brutal clarity during the heavy raids over London in the autumn and winter of 1940. Fires which could have been smothered in their early stages by a quick-witted child developed into infernos requiring the attendance of a small army of firefighters. Herbert Morrison noted the lesson and, on 31 December of the same year, announced that compulsory firewatching would be introduced. Every man who worked less than sixty hours per week, and was not already engaged in Home Guard or Civil Defence activities would thereafter be expected to put in at least forty-eight hours per month firewatching. Women who worked less than fifty-five hours a week were similarly compelled to enrol themselves.

The day-to-day organising of firewatching was the responsibility of the owners or occupiers of the buildings to be guarded. In the case of shops and offices the firewatchers, usually drawn from members of the staff, came on duty when the building closed for the night. A rest-room was provided and the duty of

43

the watchers was to ensure that all firefighting equipment was intact, and to patrol the building during air-raid alerts. It is difficult to account for the widespread dislike—and, hence, widespread dodging—of firewatching duties. Firewatching during the height of a raid was doubtless unpleasant, but was certainly no more dangerous than the work undertaken by other members of the Civil Defence forces or, for that matter, no more dangerous than living in the neighbouring houses. The unduly sensitive might perhaps dislike patrolling a gloomy, deserted building after dark but that was the major hazard likely to be encountered by most firewatchers. After the peak period of raids, the majority were able to spend the greater part of their duty period in bed—even if it were only a camp bed. The dislike may have arisen out of the traditional boss/worker antagonism. In Liverpool Ellen Wilkinson was asked some sharp questions on the so-called 'Funk Express'—the train which nightly carried wealthy businessmen out of the city while employees guarded their premises. But the lethargy was widespread. Residential areas were supposed to organise rotas of watchers to patrol the local streets and empty houses. In theory the compulsory enrolment produced an army of six million firewatchers; in practice, they were rarely seen abroad even when dignified by the name of Fire Guard and supplied with armlets and helmets.

'I object to firewatching as it appears to me to be an attempt to prevent the fulfilment of the Scripture which says that the world will be destroyed by fire.' So argued a citizen when prosecuted for failing to enrol. The argument was based on logic taken to the point of lunacy but it illustrated the dilemma of the person who, in an era of total war, was impelled by conscience to stand outside the conflict. In the First World War the problem was largely confined to men of military age who did not want to kill another human being. In the Second, when conscription applied even to women up to the age of fifty-five, potentially it affected the entire adult population. The State, too, widened the problem for the individual by adopting a more liberal attitude to conscientious objectors and recognising objections made on philosophical and even political grounds as well as those based on formal religion. The change in attitude was exactly reflected by the increase in numbers: in the First

Women ambulance drivers wait for orders

Members of the WVS checking clothes and boots sent from the U.S for distribution to blitzed families

World War there had been only 15,000 claiming exemption on grounds of conscience; in the Second there were nearly 60,000, 2,000 of whom were women.

The man or woman who wanted exemption had to persuade a tribunal that his or her motives were genuine and not simply inspired by a desire to escape the common responsibility for the common defence. The tribunals differed from those of the First World War in that no representative of the War Office sat on the bench—a significant change. The chairman of each had to be a county-court judge but the other members came from a wide cross-section of the community: in general, they were the kind of people who sat upon a magistrate's bench in peacetime. But now they were being called upon not to pronounce upon matters of fact—whether such and such a person was drunk in a public place, or had violated a traffic regulation—but to probe deep into the recesses of the human soul. And the person standing before them was forced to defend motives which, for most people, remain cloudily undefined. The State might be more liberal, but the tribunals were considerably more subtle. In place of the old conundrum—What would you do if you saw a Hun raping your sister?—the objector was asked a series of questions which forced him to define his role in a democracy at war. Had he given up drinking tea, coffee, cocoa, all of which had been brought into the country by armed convoys? Would he succour a child injured in an air-raid? If so, he was conceivably releasing a medical orderly who might be instrumental in restoring a soldier to battle conditions. Did he obey the blackout regulations—and thereby assist the country's ability to resist? Did he buy any taxed goods—and thereby contribute to the war treasury? Did he grow his own vegetables—and thereby release shipping space for arms?

It was logically impossible for any honest person to answer the questions favourably. But the tribunals, while not exactly sympathetic, did their best to interpret both the spirit and the letter of the paradoxical law which demanded that the members of a democracy should be free to refuse to defend that democracy. The role of the tribunals was, essentially, to weed out the obvious shirkers: 10,000 of these were sent packing; 5,000 of these were later prosecuted, and most of them sent to prison, for refusing to register. Of the rest, 2,900 were given unconditional exemption—the tribunals in their case recognising a genuine and irresolveable conflict of conscience, while the vast majority—40,000—were given exemption provided that they took up employment—such as forestry or agriculture—which only a fanatic could claim was directly related to the war effort.

Further Reading
Peter Fleming's *Invasion 1940* (1957) and E. S. Turner's *The Phoney War* covers the period up to autumn 1940. Charles Graves' *The Home Guard* (1943), contains copious primary material from unit histories. For the domestic problems involved see *Home Office: The Protection of your home against air raids*. Sir Aylmer Firebrace's *Fire Service Memoires* is a lively, semi-official history of the wartime fire services. Denis Haye's *Challenge of Conscience* (1949), deals with the problem of the Conscientious Objectors.

III

Total War

'The decision regarding attack on London rests with me,' Adolph Hitler informed his chiefs of staff in his first War Directive. At the end of December 1939 he repeated the statement, confident that the looming terror of mass bombardment would economically stifle the feeble British will to resist. The war was nearly a year old when the decision was taken out of his hands by a tiny number of Luftwaffe aircrew. On the night of 24 August 1940 a handful of German planes jettisoned their bombs, believing that they were either over the sea or over open country. They were, in fact, approximately over central London.

On the following night, eighty-one aircraft of Bomber Command flew to Berlin and dropped bombs in reprisal. This attack, and the half dozen which backed it up over the following week, was a pinprick compared to the appalling onslaught on Berlin three years later. But it was the first time that war had come to the capital of the Reich: honour and domestic politics demanded reprisals. Late on the afternoon of 6 September the first wave of Heinkels and Dorniers took off from French airfields and crossed the Channel. London was about to be added to the list which ran, inexorably, from Guernica via Dresden to Hiroshima.

The people of South-East England were already only too familiar with the slender 'flying pencil' shape of the Dornier and the squatter Heinkel: school-children already possessed impressive collections of 'shrapnel'—the jagged fragments of anti-aircraft shells, frequently harvested when they were still hot to the touch; the crushed wreckages of aircraft were already piled high in scores of dumps. On 16 July Hitler had decreed that preparations should be put in hand for *Operation Sealion*, the long-delayed invasion of Britain, and the Luftwaffe was ordered to the task of destroying the Royal Air Force as an essential preliminary. With admirable precision 13 August was marked down as Eagle Day—the day on which the actual destruction would begin. Later, there was to be mild academic controversy over the dates of this 'Battle of Britain', for there was no sudden, dramatic onslaught but rather a steadily increasing pressure, culminating on 15 August when 1,790 enemy aircraft were in the air over South-East England.

'There is something unreal about this air war over Britain,' Ed Murrow told his American listeners. 'Much of it you can't see, but the aircraft are up in the clouds, out of sight. Even when the Germans come down to bomb an airfield it's all over in an incredibly short space of time. You just see a bomber slanting down towards his target: three or four little things that look like marbles fall out, and it seems to take a long time for those bombs to hit the ground.' Away from the airfields that were now the primary targets, the civilian experience of the battle was of the twisting vapour trails high overhead, an occasional glint of silver as the sun caught a manoeuvring aircraft, a sudden roar of engines and clatter of machine-guns as embattled aircraft momentarily swept low.

The fighter pilots emerged as the new heroes in an ancient tradition. During the battle of France and the evacuation from Dunkirk they had been leashed in by their commander, Air Chief Marshal Dowding, for precisely this eventuality. His strategic foresight in conserving irreplaceable pilots and aircraft probably saved Britain—but it made Fighter Command one of the least popular services during the first year of the war. The average soldier, cowering in the sands of Dunkirk while Messerschmits swept unimpeded overhead, had not been in the ideal position to reflect on overall aerial strategy. RAF pilots justly resented the bitter accusations of incompetence or cowardice that were hurled at them and brawls in public houses between airmen and soldiers marred the national euphoria of the successful evacuation. Three months later, however, Winston Churchill's rotund phrase, recording the debt of the many to the few, wiped out the memory and put in

Incident, London. All visible faces bear an expression of profound shock.

its place the memory of another Thermopylae.

The public now went to the opposite extreme, encouraged by the Air Ministry's curiously inaccurate statements of enemy losses. The news-vendors of London, duly exercising cockney wit, turned the bloody encounters into a species of cricket match with their chalked headlines reading 'Score 100 to 30: England not out' or some such version. The margin was wide—but not nearly so wide as the official figures claimed. The peak raid on 15 August produced a total of seventy-six German losses for thirty-four British: the figures claimed 182 German aircraft certainly destroyed and another fifty-three 'probables'. Considering that the majority of aircraft crashed over land, it should have been a relatively simple matter to count the carcases and so arrive at a reasonably accurate assessment of enemy losses. But as the RAF's historian subsequently pointed out the error 'had an important psychological effect during the battle. For it undoubtedly inspired not only the fighter pilots but the whole nation to still greater miracles of effort.'

But though the public, from their ringside seats, might cheer the 'long-haired boys' on and make the Spitfire the national symbol of lighthearted resistance, the Chiefs of Air Staff were aware that attrition alone must inevitably bring about the destruction of Fighter Command. Then, as a result of that accidental bombing of London on 24 August, the main enemy attack was switched from military targets to civilian, psychology taking the place of strategy.

Over the next four and a half years enemy raids over Britain rose and fell in a series of great waves. The first extended from September 1940 to May 1941, including what was to be known as the London Blitz, and the attack on the major provincial centres, beginning with Coventry in November. There followed a comparative lull until the spring of 1942 when the so-called Baedekker raids ushered in a year-long period of minor, sporadic raids—'tip and run' raids—across the country. In early 1944 there was another massive attack on London, followed, on 12 June, by the first flying bomb. From June to mid-August 8,000 of these bombs were launched against Britain, 5,000 of them falling on London and the South-East. The rocket period extended from 8 September to 27 March 1945, during which 1,054 fell and on 29 March 1945 occurred the

Morning after the Blitz

last action of the war on British soil when a single flying bomb fell in Hertfordshire.

London was the dominant target throughout, paying the military price for its social dominance. Almost half of the 60,595 civilian dead were killed in the London region. The maximum tonnage of high explosives dropped on any provincial city was 2,000: London received more than 12,000 tons. It was bombed continuously for a far greater period than any other city, being raided for seventy-six consecutive nights, with only one exception, in the autumn of 1940 when a total of 8,000 tons were dropped. Sixty per cent of all houses damaged or destroyed by enemy action were the homes of Londoners: in Central London only one house in ten escaped damage. Time was to reduce the scale of London's ordeal for it was later measured against that produced by the apocalyptic bombing of Germany: the death-roll in Hamburg alone equalled that for all Britain while that of Dresden was probably three times as

51

great. But London was the first great city to be subjected to continual and heavy bombardment while still acting as the directing centre of a nation at war. The lesson learned was that the human spirit had seemingly infinite powers of adaptation. The more facile journalism of the period dramatised and vulgarised that capacity: judging by some of the newspaper reports every little old lady dragged out of some horrific situation had a merry quip on her lips. 'London can take it,' the propagandists boasted as though a ton of high explosives was an unpleasant but bracing medicine. The tawdry rhetoric, however, covered a basic truth. Somewhat to their astonishment, a random collection of human beings found that they could endure the utmost in violence and terror that other human beings could direct against them.

Officialdom had thought otherwise. In attempting to forecast Armageddon, the experts had predicted that, in addition to the tens of thousands of corpses, there would be tens of thousands—perhaps even millions—of fear-maddened people. It was not an unwarrantable assumption. Hitherto, violence had been directed almost exclusively against soldiers—resilient young males, bound together by military discipline and able to purge fear by taking violent action in their own turn. Violence now was directed against the very young and the very old; against women; against the mentally and physically sick. It was unpredictable, erupting in the midst of humdrum, domestic circumstances. It was unopposable. Yet, incredibly, instead of the outbreaks of mass hysteria expected, there was, in fact, a statistical decline in neurotic disorders; there were fewer suicides; the incidence of drunkenness—constant index of social instability—declined by a remarkable fifty per cent. It would seem that normal conditions in a great city were far more taxing on the individual than the most violent abnormality.

The most radical social change was the spirit of comradeship fostered by mutual danger, producing the extraordinary spectacle of the British actually speaking to each other without being introduced. It was impossible to maintain the traditional British reserve, to cherish the much-loved class distinctions under conditions of enforced intimacy. London, notorious for its unfriendliness even in a nation which elevated privacy into a moral code, was composed now of thousands of interlocking

ARP rest centre for the homeless, Plymouth

groups—groups in shelters whiling the long hours away with conversation and informal entertainment; groups working desperately in the ruins of a shattered home seeking the life that might remain; groups seeking and giving information and aid; groups in wardens posts; groups firewatching in deserted, gloomy buildings. The average citizen found himself sustained as part of a purposive community, after perhaps spending a lifetime of social isolation. The cameraderie weakened with the ending of the great raids and disappeared entirely, abruptly, with the coming of peace but it left behind a profound and enduring sense of nostalgia.

The first great raid, on the East End of London, was the only one which threatened to shatter the communal fabric and justify, in military terms, the use of terror as a weapon. 'Everybody is worried about the feeling in the East End,' Harold Nicolson recorded in his diary ten days after the first attack. 'There is much bitterness. It is said that even the King and Queen were booed when they visited the destroyed areas.' The dense population, crowded into flimsy houses with the minimum of space between them, were peculiarly vulnerable to aerial attack. The death roll was not particularly heavy: it was the social chaos which followed that accounted for the near revolutionary reaction. The authorities had made excellent preparations for disposing of the dead; they had not counted on being obliged to find shelter for the living, for statistics had seemed to show that the number of survivors would be in rough equilibrium with surviving accommodation. The mass evacuation scheme which should have lightened their labours had been an almost total failure: of the one-and-a-half million mothers and children who had been evacuated from London in September 1939, nearly one-and-a-quarter millions had returned. In a little over two weeks the authorities had some 25,000 homeless people on their hands. It had been calculated that the average 'bombed-out' person would spend only a matter of hours in one of the crude Rest Centres, a later survey showed that people were living in them for periods of ten days and more.

A Red Cross worker reported the conditions in one of these Rest Centres—an elementary school in Stepney—which was housing some 300 people. They slept on the floor in the midst of their possessions, their only sanitary arrangement consisting of ten pails and coal scuttles. 'By the middle of the night these containers overflow so that, as the night advances, urine and faeces spread in ever increasing volume over the floor. The space is narrow so that whoever enters inevitably steps in the sewage and carries it on his shoes all over the building.' Disorder inevitably produced tragedy in its turn. In West Ham an unknown number of people were temporarily billeted in a school in the heart of the target area. A series of misunderstandings delayed the arrival of the coaches which should have taken them to a relatively safer area: the school was bombed and some 450 people lost their lives.

Throughout these first few days of total warfare the West End of London had remained comparatively unscathed. Journalists made the most of the dramatic contrast between life in the luxury hotels and conditions in the East End and a handful of Communists duly attempted to exploit the situation. On the night of 15 September a small group of East Enders, led by a Communist MP, gathered outside the Savoy Hotel, waiting for

Searchlight battery in action

the first siren of the evening. It sounded and the group entered the hotel, demanding that they should be accommodated in its luxurious deep shelter. The management was in a quandary: it was hardly possible to eject the group, one of whom was a woman in an advanced state of pregnancy but it was equally obvious that the demonstration was something less than spontaneous. The group was given shelter in the dormitory but the problem was resolved when the all-clear siren sounded, less than a quarter of an hour afterwards, and the management was able to make the legitimate demand that non-clients of the hotel should leave. The hotel was full of foreign journalists and the incident therefore received maximum coverage abroad—particularly in Germany where the 100 or so people became a panic-stricken mob on the edge of revolution—but it made little impact at home. The shifting of the attacks to the West End of London—above all, the bombing of Buckingham Palace on 15 September—gave forceful demonstration that the war was truly democratic and the embryonic revolution died.

The raids evolved a scenario of their own. The overture was the chilling rise and fall of the sirens, followed shortly afterwards by the uneven drone of bomber engines. People grew to hate that sound even more than the sound of explosions, for it seemed filled with a personal malignancy: most claimed to be able to detect the difference in sound between 'one of theirs' and 'one of ours'. The path of the bombers was marked by the stabbing beams of searchlights, bars of so intense a light that they seemed solid, sweeping backwards and forwards until one had pinned an aircraft against the night sky and then was joined by others like a hunting pack. The arrival of aircraft over the target was marked by a spectacular display of lights, ominous portents which yet had great beauty about them. The novelist R. H. Mottram described how the attack on Norwich 'was heralded by means of parachute flares that lit up the old city as it had not been during darkness since the firework display and bonfire of Queen Victoria's diamond Jubilee in 1897'. Moonlight provided the best conditions for attack and the term 'bomber's moon' ousted 'lover's moon' for the duration of the war. But even on moonless nights the blazing chandeliers of flares, hung like fiery fruit in the sky, cancelled what protection darkness might give.

By the time they had burned themselves out, the first bombs had arrived, signalling their approach by a terrifying shriek; a few were fitted with whistles or sirens to increase the psychological effect. People living in the vicinity of a falling bomb noticed that electric lights dipped and wavered a fraction of a second before it struck. A macabre new guessing game arose from the fact that the bombs fell in series of sticks: straining ears would follow the explosions and try to estimate where the next one would occur. It was commonly believed that the bomb which killed was never heard.

The bombs used in the early part of the war were comparatively small, the maximum being some 500 pounds in weight. Mingled with them, however, was a terrifying weapon which was commonly referred to as a land-mine. It was, in fact, an ordinary sea-mine but its gigantic size—over eight feet in length—and the fact that it descended absolutely silently by parachute gave it a peculiarly unnerving reputation. Gerald Henderson, the sub-Librarian of St Paul's, described one which fell on the site of St Paul's Cross and failed to explode. It was still draped with its parachute and he thought, at first, that 'the silk might have been blown out of some warehouse. I went up to the place and drew aside the silk covering. It then appeared that the object beneath it was a shining sea-mine. It was like an inverted, elongated pear in shape and had rows of horns at the top and bottom. It had dropped perpendicularly and, most fortunately, had remained in that posture.' If the mine had, in fact, toppled over on to one of its horns then the greater part of St Paul's Cathedral would have been destroyed. Mines were not only larger than bombs but, because they exploded on the surface and not after burying themselves, their lateral destructive force was greater.

The giant, striding explosions of high-explosive bombs was war made evident and dramatic; the fall of incendiaries was totally unimpressive, the sound they made being variously described as a 'plopping' or 'rattling' as they hit the ground. The public was slow to appreciate the full implications of this apparently insignificant weapon. Before the raids began Mass Observation reported that only a third of the people they had interviewed were aware of the simple official instructions as to how to deal with them. Some of the replies given were of an astonishing naievety—unless, perhaps, the observer's leg was being pulled. 'Sit back and hold tight.' 'Leave it to a Warden.' 'Put on your gas mask.' 'Leave it where it was and run.' The observer remarked that the commonest answer was that the bomb should be put in water, or water thrown on the bomb— either method likely to be fatal, for, as millions of ARP leaflets had stressed, 'if you throw a bucket of water on a burning incendiary bomb, it will explode and throw burning fragments in all directions.'

The training field of hard experience, however, produced thousands of highly efficient amateur firefighting teams. Their equipment could not have been simpler, consisting as it did of

Fire fighters   *September 1940: fires in London Docks*

bags or buckets of sand, and the stirrup pump operated by two people. One did the actual pumping while the other crawled along the floor, dragging the length of hosing with him and directing a fine spray at the bomb. Each pump cost about £1 to produce and was undoubtedly one of the more profitable investments.

Sir Aylmer Firebrace, chief and, later, historian of the London Fire Brigade, vividly described what happened when a fire grew out of control. The fire took place in the Surrey Docks, the biggest fire on the night of 7 September 1940, 'immense in its area, moving with disconcerting speed, generating terrific heat. It set alight the wooden blocks in the roadway, a thing without precedent. A blaze covering such an area is not only worse than a smaller one in direct proportion to its area, but is far harder to fight than its mere extent would suggest. The greater the cumulative heat, the fiercer the draught of cold air dragged in to feed it, and thus the quicker the movement of the fire and the greater the length of its flames. They were so long and their heat so great as to blister the paint on fireboats that tried to slip past under the lee of the opposite bank 300 yards away. Solid embers a foot long were tossed into streets far off to start fresh fires.'

Firemen in the Docks became connoisseurs of fire. 'There were rum fires, with torrents of blazing liquid and barrels exploding like bombs themselves. There was a paint fire, another cascade of white hot flame, coating the pumps with varnish that could not be cleaned for weeks. A rubber fire gave forth black clouds of smoke so asphyxiating that it could only be fought from a distance. Sugar, it seems, burns well in liquid form as it floats on the water. Tea makes a blaze that is "sweet, sickly and very intense".'

Bomb blast was capricious in effect, its lethality modified by scores of unpredictable factors so that the same bomb could demolish a five-storey building and leave a human being unharmed—but stripped naked. Glass fragments proved to be a vicious and ubiquitous weapon, killing and maiming hundreds who would otherwise have escaped unhurt. The effect could be reduced by sticking strips of tape or even paper on the glass, and most of the windows in Central London were so adorned. But they could still explode like a bomb, the fragments lacerat-

*The capriciousness of blast: furniture and clothing on
the upper floor have been untouched by the explosion*

ing. After the first heavy raids the roads and pavements were
covered as though with a frost with broken glass, producing an
excruciating sensation for those who had to walk over it. The
effect declined, however, as the numbers of windows declined:
shop fronts were boarded in, the lethal area of plate being replaced by a peephole. Goods were in short supply by that time
so that the loss of display space was, if anything, welcome to the
shopkeeper.

Dirt was one of the odder side-effects of blast. Dust and
debris that had been accumulating for years, or even centuries,
beneath floorboards, in attics and countless crevices was sud-
denly expelled with enormous violence to settle slowly for hours
afterwards. When a coal dump was hit by a high explosive bomb
people over a wide radius were covered with a layer of pulver-

ised coal-dust. The first need after a raid was a good wash, a need only too often denied through a widespread lack of water, so that sheer discomfort was one of the more common memories. There was, too, a unique 'blitz' smell—a compound of charred timber and domestic gas: of the stench of a water-doused fire and the aftermath of high-explosive—its constituents varying from locality to locality but, once smelled, never forgotten.

In street after street the Englishman's castle, so long inviolate to prying eyes, now displayed its pathetic secrets to the world. Observer after observer remarked on the infinite poignancy of these shattered homes: the lovingly-chosen wallpaper of one room clashing with that in what remained of the next: the shabby look of furniture in full daylight: the expediencies of poverty betrayed. In this matter, however, there was equality for the most richly furnished home looked as much a rubbish heap as the poorest after it had been hit by a bomb.

It was this curious, rubbishy look that probably led to much of the looting that took place after raids. In some instances looting was undoubtedly organised: the ghouls who crept into the Café de Paris and stripped jewellery and wallets from the dead were certainly working to a system they had used before. They appeared immediately after the bomb had exploded and left immediately before the Civil Defence workers arrived. But most looting was spontaneous—and trivial, as Ed Murrow noted. 'Many of the articles picked up from the bombed houses are of little intrinsic value, a book or a piece of ribbon or a bucketful of coal—that sort of thing. Many people convicted of looting are certainly not criminal types and have not taken the objects for reasons of personal gain. One has a strange feeling—or at least I have—in looking at the contents of a bombed house or shop, that the things scattered about don't belong to anyone.'

A survey undertaken in London in the November of 1940 disclosed a remarkable fact: only forty per cent of the population regularly went to a shelter at night during an air raid—and this was in the earlier period when familiarity had not dulled the terrors of attack. The majority of the population under attack seems to have gone to bed as though nothing untoward were happening, or was likely to happen—a statistical demon-

stration of the power of sheer habit and of an ingrained opti-
mism that seems indistinguishable from fatalism.

There was, however, a powerful reason for risking death in
the comfort of one's own bed: the majority of those who used
shelters went into an Anderson shelter. And an Anderson
shelter on a winter's night was an extremely unpleasant
experience. The fragile-looking structures proved highly
competent for their primary task of protecting life from a
violent end: they could survive almost anything except a
direct hit. But even official and private ingenuity could make
of them nothing more than a steel shell sunk in the damp earth.
Opinion was divided as to whether it was better to go to bed in
the shelter as a matter of course every night, or wait until there
was an alert. The latter course ensured a decent night's sleep if
there was, in fact, no alert. But if the siren sounded there was
the nightmarish business of struggling into clothes, grabbing
essentials and running out into any of the extremes of an
English winter night. In 1940 the new Home Secretary,
Herbert Morrison, initiated the designing of a shelter which
should give most of the protection of an Anderson without its
disadvantages. The shelter, inevitably called the 'Morrison',
was designed to be erected in the house itself. It resembled a
massive steel table—it was, indeed, usually used as a table for it
took up a large part of the average-sized room, squeezing out
most of the furniture. A wire-mesh strung a few inches up from

*Adapted basement shelter: this is probably being used by the staff
of offices and shops above*

Street shelter: the least popular kind of shelter

the bottom made a reasonably comfortable bed, and more mesh at the sides protected the occupants from falling rubble. Even if the house collapsed, the Morrison usually survived, providing a kind of cave in the heart of the ruins. Like the Anderson, the Morrison was issued free to those earning less than £350 a year, and at a cost of £7 to those earning more; by the end of the war more than a million of them were in use.

Only nine per cent of the population used public shelters. On the night of 10 September 1940 Ed Murrow drove round London, inspecting the different kinds of shelter life. 'We found, like everything else in this world, the kind of protection you get from bombs depends on how much money you have. On the other hand, the most expensive dwelling places here do not necessarily provide the best shelters, but certainly they are the most comfortable. We looked in on a renowned Mayfair hotel and found many old dowagers and retired colonels settling back on the overstuffed settees in the lobby. It wasn't the sort of protection I'd seek from a half-ton bomb, but if you were a retired colonel and his lady you might feel that the risk was worthwhile because you would at least be bombed with the right sort of people. . . . Only a couple of blocks away we pushed aside the canvas curtain of a trench cut out of the lawn of a London park. Inside were half a hundred people, some of them stretched out on the hard wooden benches. The rest huddled over in their overcoats and blankets. Dimmed electric lights glowed on the whitewashed walls and the cannonade of anti-aircraft and reverberation of the big stuff the Germans were dropping rattled the dustboards under foot at intervals.'

Trench shelters were even more liable to flood than Andersons: one observer recorded how he sat throughout a raid with stinking water lapping almost up to his knees. Nevertheless, trenches were more popular than the brick surface shelters which began to appear in large numbers in the winter of 1939–40. These were intended not only for passers-by caught in a raid, but also for those many localities whose houses did not possess gardens for the erection of an Anderson. Surface shelters were simply brick boxes with an immense slab of concrete for a roof and an error in building specifications made deathtraps of many of those built in early 1940. The proportion of cement in the mortar was disastrously reduced—in some cases eliminated altogether—the bricks being held together only by a mixture of lime and sand. Blast easily ruptured the flimsy structures, bringing down the solid roof to crush those inside. Even when the error was corrected by building a curtain wall all round and extending the roof so that it overlapped the walls, the shelters remained unpopular. Inside they were at once cold and stuffy; frequently they stank, being used as unofficial urinals during the day. The only furnishing was a wooden bench running along the unplastered walls; the lighting was insufficient for reading. Altogether the surface shelters combined the minimum of protection with the maximum of boredom and discomfort.

In addition to the official shelters were the uncountable number of refuges which the people found for themselves, or were evolved under need. Continual needling by the Press resulted in the reinforcement, and opening, of scores of basements in the massive Victorian and Edwardian buildings in the City of London. Certain buildings became popular less because of their intrinsic safety than because they had developed into a species of communal centre, offering the illusion of safety in numbers. The so-called Tilbury shelter in Stepney acquired a Hogarthian reputation. It consisted of an immense complex of arches and vaults under the railway at Stepney and had been used as a shelter in the First World War. The local council had taken over part of it and made an official shelter housing at least 3,000 people but even this number was dwarfed by those flooding into the unofficial—and unreinforced—section. It was estimated that as many as 16,000 people crowded into an area that was still being used as a food warehouse. The resulting sanitary conditions were unspeakable, the results of a direct hit unthinkable. Nevertheless, people queued for hours for the privilege of obtaining a few square feet of filthy ground, and of sharing in the feverish social life that came to characterise the shelter. Situated as it was in the heart of Dockland, it was used by people of a dozen different races and seemingly every possible colour combination, each race contributing its customs to the whole. Hawkers and prostitutes plied their wares; spontaneous dances and sing-songs sprang into being. Respectable families slept as best they could in the midst of drunken brawls. Tilbury shelter was irredeemably squalid; morally reprehensible; physically dangerous—yet it is wholly understandable why thousands flocked to it instead of sitting out the weary watches in some cold, gloomy, deserted brick shelter.

The smallest percentage of shelterers were those who left the most vivid memory in the popular mind. Only 12,000 people used the Tubes, barely four per cent of all shelterers but because of the public nature of their shelter they were seen by more people over a greater stretch of time and so came to typify the Blitz. The Government had declined to make use of the Tubes as shelters for much the same reason as it had refused to construct 'deep shelters': it feared the emergence of a 'shelter mind', the creation of a troglodyte population burrowing ever deeper away from the threat of bombs. But the underground railways—warm, well-lit, deep and accessible—were a powerful attraction and the population defeated the Government's intention by the simple device of buying the lowest-priced ticket, entering the tubes as travellers and remaining as shelterers.

A clear-cut pattern of tube life, based predominantly on family groups, rapidly emerged. During the afternoon a member of the family—usually an older child—would arrive bringing bedding or the like and use it to stake out a claim: the first choice was the platforms at the deeper levels. Bowing

Unofficial Tube shelter: settling down for the night

to the inevitable, the LPTB could at least insist that free passage be left for travellers and a white line was drawn, eight feet from the edge of the platform, beyond which bedding could not be put down until 7.30 in the evening.

The rest of the family would arrive when the normal day's work was ended, bringing with them food and drink for the night and additional bedding. Most groups used the same tube station night after night, forming a community of their own. People tended to settle down early for the night out of sheer boredom, but there was little sleep until 10.30 when the trains stopped.

After the rush-hour had ended at 7.30 the bedding area was extended up to four feet from the platform edge and this was the last opportunity for late comers to find a place. Thereafter those who arrived settled as best they could in the approach passages, on the stairs and even between the lines after the electric current had been switched off. It says much for the unconscious coordination behind this whole extraordinary way of life that no one was actually electrocuted by bedding down even a second too early. Most people left long before the current was switched on. The All Clear usually sounded before 6 a.m. and by seven o'clock the tubes were back to normal—except for the mounds of rubbish, including human excrement, to be cleared away by the depleted station staffs. There was little temptation to linger in these draughty, smelly, lice-infested caverns. In some few localities—notably the dead end of the Liverpool Street extension, bombed-out families made semi-permanent homes, but the vast majority of people used them simply during the night raids. Not all the Tubes were as safe as they appeared: the older ones, in particular, ran just below the surface and were little more bomb-proof than an ordinary cellar. Bombs did occasionally penetrate, the most terrible occurrence taking place at Balham station. An estimated 600 people were sheltering there when a bomb tore through the roof, shattering a water-main so that those who survived the effect of the bomb blast were swept away and drowned.

The singing, steady note of the All Clear brought a temporary sense of euphoria but for thousands it also heralded a night-marish period. These were the people who returned to their homes and found a heap of rubble—the 'bombed out'. The shock of the loss of a home, the sudden destruction of something that had been built up over a lifetime, could cause temporary amnesia: the victims would wander in a daze or try and retrieve some totally useless object—a battered bird cage, a handful of ribbons, a broken picture frame. The shock gave way to the humdrum, all-absorbing problem of how to carry on the business of living without its necessities: where to find saucepans to cook in and a fire to put them on: where to find a change of clothing; where to bath the baby—and how to feed it. Very few people indeed had any reserves of money to make good such a domestic cataclysm; the wise took their cash with them into the shelters but this rarely amounted to more than the few shillings set aside for day to day expenditure. And, even if they had money, the goods necessary to set up a home were just not available. Rationing and registration created another problem. In some cases it was necessary to visit half a dozen government offices in order to collect the necessary documents —trudging perhaps miles during the course of the day. And above all there was the necessity to find four walls and a roof for the coming night.

Throughout the United Kingdom as a whole two-and-a-quarter million people faced this problem during 1940 and 1941: in the London region one person in every six was engaged, over the same period, in the demoralising search for a home. The social problem of the Rest Centres assumed enormous proportions. Officially, a centre was supposed merely to act as a clearing house—a place where a family could perhaps wash and change and collect themselves before looking for a home: the official mind was so firmly wedded to this concept that the authorities refused to supply blankets for fear that the centres might become too comfortable and tempt the families to stay. In practice, the centres became miniature refugee camps. The burden fell most heavily upon women— particularly upon those whose husbands were absent in the Forces or on war work. Men who worked in the locality might take a day or so off to establish their families somewhere but thereafter their wives were alone day after day, coping with the almost impossible task of keeping the family together under conditions of increasing squalor. The fact that the centres functioned at all was due entirely to an army of voluntary

Rehabilitation centre in converted dance hall

workers, some of them defying government edicts, technically breaking the law to supply their charges with bedding and fuel and food. The formal organisations, in particular the WVS, formed the backbone of this army but human need again and again produced the human reaction of spontaneous succour. Richard Titmuss records the activities of one such Samaritan — an epic figure, identified only as 'Mrs B' who was a beetroot seller in Islington market. 'When the raids started she walked into Ritchie Street rest centre and took charge. She found a supply of milk for the babies, bedded them down early with their mothers, and administered powders. Then she put the oldest and feeblest on the remaining beds and benches and had the whole household, one hundred to three hundred in all, asleep or quiet as the bombs came whining down. In the morning she organised the washing, bathed the babies, swept the floors, supervised breakfast, and went home about eleven o'clock to sleep (or sell beetroots?). In the evening she was back again. She made one rest centre a place of security, order and decency for hundreds of homeless people.'

The bombed-out possessed, at least, a direct claim for official assistance; those who were rendered homeless by unexploded bombs existed in a kind of limbo. By the end of November 1940 there were at least 3,000 bombs lying around London: a few were delayed action weapons, the majority were probably duds but, perforce, all were treated as potential dangers and a wide area around each was evacuated until it could be dealt with. The residents in these areas were rendered as effectively, if temporarily, homeless as if their homes had actually been destroyed, but technically they had no claim.

The fantastic mosaic of local government added its own inimitable quota to the chaos: in London alone there were ninety-six authorities—legal, administrative, charitable, police and the rest and the citizen in search of aid only too often found himself passed from one to the other. In the absence of a coherent system, the victim was forced to turn to the coldest of charities, the Poor Law authorities, and found that a system designed to protect nineteenth-century ratepayers was vigorously flourishing in the midst of twentieth-century total war. Traditionally, the poor of a given locality were supported by ratepayers in that locality. Local authorities were therefore supposed to distinguish between their own 'native' homeless, and otherwise identical people who happened to come from another locality—perhaps only a street away.

Malcolm Macdonald, the Minister of Health, resolved the impossible situation, adopting the Prime Minister's own sweeping approach to national problems. Shortly after the major raids began in London he promised Treasury backing to any measures that the London County Council considered necessary and in February 1941 the policy was extended to all local authorities in the United Kingdom. Now that individual goodwill was backed by the power of the State, the lunatic chaos was ended in a remarkably brief space of time. 'Moreover, what had been done was done, not in peaceful conditions, not when supplies were plentiful but at a time when administrators and executive officers could have found plentiful excuses for inaction. But this was a period in the social history of London

The destruction of Coventry

when most men and women would have found it intolerable to trade in excuses.'

On 14 November 1940, 330 bombers raided Coventry for eleven hours, killing 554 people, adding the new word 'coventration' to wartime language, and heralding an era of universal fear for the whole country. The scenes in London were repeated again and again, differing only in scale. Again the bombers found populations who were unprepared, despite the horrific example of London. The tangle of local authority responsibilities, the traditional municipal jealousy of Whitehall retarded Civil Defence measures. In some areas the projected relationship between town hall and Regional Commissioner worked ideally. Bernard Storey, Town Clerk of Norwich, recorded one such example of sensible cooperation. 'Plans had been made for organised military aid in case of need. An elaborate system of code telephone messages *must* always be used in the sacred name of security. In the event it boiled down to a simple telephone call: "Do you want any help, Storey? Right, I'll be down in my car in five minutes."' In other areas municipal pride and stubbornness imperilled—indeed, actually cost—lives. 'The local authorities almost always made the mistake of not calling

70

for help soon enough,' Richard Titmuss noted in his official history of the social services. 'Sometimes the regional officers also gained an impression, when they arrived at the scene, that their help was not really welcomed.'

The provincial raids produced a phenomenon that was so widespread, so clearly defined that it earned a name—'trekking'. In the evening hundreds and, in some cases, thousands of people would flock out of the city threatened with attack, travelling for distances of up to thirty miles, sleeping where they could, and returning in the morning. The phenomenon was first noticed in Plymouth, which was heavily raided on two successive nights in March 1941 and again on five occasions in April. A total of 30,000 people were rendered homeless, but something in the region of 50,000 people left the city at nightfall during the second half of April and the beginning of May. 'Tonight, some of the city's streets are nothing more than a desert of dusty rubble. They are streets that the citizens leave for the countryside when night falls,' the *Plymouth Evening Herald* wrote on 1 May. The fortunate few found shelter with friends or relatives in the neighbouring villages; the majority slept where they could as far away as they could get. A spontaneous carrier service came into being: coalmen, farmers, milkmen leaving the city at night would pass some recognised point and pick up the trekkers. Policemen bent the law, stopping drivers and persuading them to give lifts.

The phenomenon spread as city after city was attacked during 1941. Initially, the government was reluctant to increase and improve the rural rest centres, fearful of encouraging the movement. But again common sense overcame theory and by the early summer of 1941 improvements similar to those made

Crashed Dornier bomber

in London were under way throughout the country. The need, however, had largely passed with the ending of the heavy raids but for a few months Britain had had a brief vision of something with which the Continent was only too familiar—the tragic spectacle of refugees trudging inhospitable roads.

The tip-and-run raids which followed were individually unimportant but in their sum they contributed substantially to loss of production and general war weariness. Urban life was brought to an abrupt halt by the threatened approach of a small force of raiders. The warning might sound two or three times a day, sending thousands into shelters, emptying the streets, halting production in the war factories—and the raiders might, after all, bypass the city altogether. A new form of warning was adopted. The sirens still sounded, giving warning that enemy aircraft were in the vicinity but ordinary life

The miraculous survival of St Paul's is made evident after the rubble has been cleared away

continued. Meanwhile spotters, nicknamed Jim Crows, were stationed on roofs and on the indubitable approach of bombers, would sound the 'crash warning'—a series of staccato blasts on klaxon horns. The horrendous, blaring noise probably caused quite a few heart attacks but it gave the necessary few seconds warning to take shelter before the bombers were actually overhead.

For most people the tip-and-run raids of 1942–43 were the last rolls of thunder of a receding storm. But in South-East England, and particularly London, the storm returned in 1944 in a peculiarly terrorising form. The two 'Vengeance Weapons' of the concluding months of the war did not so much mark an end, as give an unpleasant foretaste of the possibilities of a new kind of war. Significantly, perhaps, there were nicknames for the V1 or flying bomb—the excruciating punning of 'Bob Hopes' (Bob down and hope for the best) ; buzz bomb, derived from the sound of the roaring exhaust or, more commonly, doodlebug, presumably from its unpredictable nature. There were, however, no nicknames for the V2, the weapon which signified its existence only by a titanic explosion. The peak of the flying bomb raids occurred between June and August: at one period they were arriving off the coast of Britain at the rate of a hundred a day. The overall effects of the raids were small compared with the mass piloted raids of earlier years; locally, their effect was terrible for each bomb weighed a ton and exploded immediately on impact. The psychological effect was, if anything, worse. Along the entire flight path of the machine people would 'freeze up inside' as a CD worker put it, waiting in an agony of expectation for the snarling roar to cease abruptly, immediately heralding the fall to earth. They were denied even the release of vicariously fighting back, for a flying bomb that was shot down was precisely as lethal as one which crashed when its fuel ran out. Approximately half of them were shot down over the sea or over open country, but the half which got through the outer defences killed and seriously injured more than 24,000 people.

The advancing Allied Armies in France overran the launching sites and the numbers of flying bombs rapidly fell off after August. But on 8 September the first of the long-range rockets fell on the borough of Chiswick. Death now struck without any

Business as usual

warning whatsoever for the flash and supersonic bang marking the arrival of the rocket overhead virtually coincided with the roar of the explosion. One of the few cartoons inspired by the rockets had a bored layman retorting to an expert: 'Then I suppose you hear the squeak of their fountain pens as they design the beastly thing.' The proportion of rockets to flying bombs was barely one to eight, but each killed and injured twice as many people on average. Probably the worst incident took place in Deptford where a rocket, falling into a crowd of shoppers, caused nearly 300 casualties.

The solitary explosion in Ditchingfield, Hertfordshire on 29 March 1945 marked the end of five years of aerial warfare over Britain. The enemy had dropped a grand total of 70,995 tons of high explosive and uncountable thousands of incendiaries, killing 60,595 civilians and seriously injuring another 86,182, destroying 222,000 homes and damaging nearly five million more.

Further Reading
The vast majority of material on the Blitzes relates almost exclusively to London. Constantine Fitzgibbon's *The Blitz* (1957), concentrates on the early period with invaluable firsthand accounts of 'incidents'. John Strachey's *Post D* tells the story of one ARP warden's post. Doreen Idle's *War Over West Ham* (1943) and W. R. Matthews' *St Paul's Cathedral in war-time* (1946), give two out of many specific views. For a neutral's viewpoint see Ed Murrow *This is London* (1941). For social service generally see Titmuss. Outside London R. H. Mottram's *Assault upon Norwich* (1945), is a succinct account of a provincial raid, by a professional novelist.

IV

Breadcrumbs in Battledress

The war was nearly five months old before food rationing was even tentatively introduced. The delay provided yet another indication of the gap between leaders and people for the majority were not merely reconciled to the idea of rationing, but actually wanted it to be introduced as soon as possible. Their desire rose less from any fear of shortages than a belief that, in this vital matter, all should be treated equally. In the autumn of 1939 a grocer in the East End of London bitterly summed up the results of the existing 'free market'.

'It is bringing in all the rich people from the West End to take the poor people's food. I came back from lunch this morning and found a beautiful car outside. A lady and her husband were carrying twenty-eight pounds (of sugar) each—and the chauffeur twenty-eight pounds on each arm. I made them put it all back again and gave them three pounds each. I don't think that sort of thing is right—they take all the poor people's food. They don't give the poor a chance.'

That particular shopkeeper was already operating his own unofficial ration scheme. A few were already cashing in on the fear of shortages, selling at high prices to all-comers but most took the cautious, long-term view that it was better to reserve at least some stocks for their regular customers. They gained the gratitude of their regulars, but the abuse of the casual shopper. Goods for favoured customers rapidly disappeared from the open shelves, producing one of the great wartime phrases 'under the counter'. Inevitably, even justified price increases became 'profiteering'. A greengrocer complained: 'One week there was two boats of oranges sunk and that affected the

Bacon, sugar, butter were the only rationed foods when this photograph was taken in February 1940

market of course: the price went up and you can imagine the complaints.'

Ration books had been issued at the end of September but they remained unused while the War Cabinet tried to make up its collective mind. 'Oddly enough, the chief opposition to rationing was based on the view that the rations were too small —as if the Ministry of Food could vary the supplies of food at its immediate will,' the official historian later noted. Winston Churchill, then First Lord of the Admiralty, was, for once, out of step with public opinion and opposed the whole idea. The *Daily Express* backed him up. 'The public should revolt against the food rationing system, that dreadful and terrible iniquity which some of the ministers want to adopt. There is no necessity for the trouble and expense of rationing because there may be a shortage of this or that inessential commodity. Why should old women be forced to wait here and there before the shops for their supplies? This form of folly is difficult and almost impossible to understand.'

It is difficult to see how the little old lady of journalistic fancy would benefit by a free for all. But the government, prodded by public opinion and its own Minister of Food, reluctantly agreed that food rationing would start on 8 January 1940. On that grey Monday morning the dreary-looking ration book became a priceless possession. The first items rationed were bacon and ham, sugar and butter; meat followed in March, rationed by price, not by weight, and in July, fell the greatest blow of all on the British kitchen: tea was rationed to two ounces per week. Thereafter other items followed—including cheese, cooking fat, sweets, conserves—until, by 1944, eleven shillings out of every £ spent on food was expended on rationed items.

A favourite picture feature in the newspapers was a photograph of an adult's ration for a week, a ration which a moderately heavy eater might get through in a day. Members of families, particularly large families, were certainly better off than people living by themselves, for communal eating made the most of what was available. But families had their own problems. They might perhaps decide to share out the rations as they arrived, with the result that the improvident hungrily eyed their relations' supplies for the greater part of the week. Expectant mothers and children under five received certain additional foods—in particular, a supply of precious eggs. As a result of government policy of reducing animal foodstuffs in favour of direct-consumption foods, millions of hens were slaughtered in the early months of the war. Eggs were rationed to one per person per week and it took a strong-minded woman to eat her share for the sake of her unborn child with active and hungry children looking on. The day that 'the rations came' ousted payday as the major point of the week. In most households the last day of the ration week was a nightmare for the housewife and a sore trial for her family. The British passion

Ration cards for travellers, children, and adults

for strong, sweet tea resulted in bizarre experiments. The tea ration itself was just sufficient when used communally but the sugar ration was woefully inadequate. Tea was sweetened with honey, treacle, even boiled sweets. Saccharine came on the market: the tiny tablets imparted an unpleasant, metallic taste but at least gave the illusion of sweetness.

In the fruit season the housewife could take part of the family's jam ration in the form of sugar for making her own preserves. There was no check on the use, but the wise family avoided the temptation of indulging in an orgy of sweet tea: pound for pound, the sugar produced a far higher quantity of home-made jam than the ration of shop-bought jam allowed. Throughout the country women turned again to the ancient and almost forgotten craft of preserving. Experiments were made in drying plums for use as a kind of prune. Carrots, with their hint of sweetness, were particularly popular, though most discovered that the hoped-for carrot jam turned out to be a kind of chutney.

Behind the housewife was an immensely powerful organisation, a vast bureaucracy of some 50,000 civil servants which yet, miraculously, kept its finger on the public pulse—the Ministry of Food. At its head was an ex-businessman, ex-social worker, who was without doubt the best-known person in the wartime government, Winston Churchill alone excepted. Frederick Marquis, Lord Woolton, was appointed Minister of Food in April 1940 and held the highly vulnerable post for three years. His task was unglamorous, being to act as shopkeeper to the nation: his role was the most vital of the civilian ministries. Even had there been no Lord Woolton there would have been a rationing system and it would undoubtedly have worked well. But it would not have worked with the flair, the compassion and, indeed, the sense of adventure with which the Ministry of Food operated. Woolton worked on two fronts: behind the scenes was the meticulous businessman and administrator who would not assent to the rationing of a commodity unless the ration could be honoured. In front was the social worker, the enthusiastic propagandist. He believed that it was not sufficient merely to inform the housewife that such and such a commodity was now 'on the ration': she was to be helped, instructed—challenged—to make the best of what she had. The Ministry of Food poured out a steady stream of advertisements: some perky —

> *Reflect when ever you indulge*
> *It is not beautiful to bulge.*
> *A large untidy corporation*
> *Is far from helpful to the nation*

— some precise, breaking down classes of food into their constituents in language anybody could understand. Potato Pete made his bow, a cheerful, rustic figure explaining how potatoes —unrationed—did not necessarily have to be boiled to a pulp but could be made into a variety of appetising dishes. A generation of women who looked upon meat and two veg as being the ultimate in cookery were cajoled to experiment with a remarkable variety of likely—and unlikely—foods.

Woolton identified himself fully with his organisation: not his least patriotic gesture was to give his name to a dish made up out of carrots, parsnips, turnips and potatoes, covered with a most curious sauce. A BBC producer described how he prepared for one of his broadcast talks. 'Lord Woolton listens to what you say—which is by no means the same thing as saying that he accepts your advice. But if he does he acts on it gracefully: if he doesn't he has good reason for rejecting it. The way he got down to the job in the studio also appealed to me. Faced with the microphone he emptied his pockets: a pile of small change, a gold watch and some keys were placed on the table beside him. After a few minutes, in between sentences, he slipped off his coat and settled down to do a real job of work. . . . If this is the type of man selected by the present Prime Minister Britain will surely be all right—at last.'

It is difficult to say how far Woolton succeeded in educating the innately conservative British cook. As late as 1943 Mass Observation reported, in its *An Enquiry into People's Homes*: 'What emerges most significantly is an unwillingness of people to alter their eating habits in the face of food shortage. War or no war the Sunday joint still appears on every table.' The observers noted 'hardly any attempt to make more of the rations by any new type of dish, either invented or culled from hints in the Press and elsewhere'. On this viewpoint, the harassed housewife coped simply by reducing quantities. Not all the innova-

Lord Woolton addressing a meeting of the Food Committee

tions of the Ministry were successful. Whale meat met with almost universal loathing. People, perforce, had to eat the National Wholemeal Loaf in place of the favoured white bread. The courtly 'Peterborough' in the *Daily Telegraph* found that it went well 'with a glass of Fonseca 1920' but most people complained that it was like eating bran. Tuna fish was as unpopular as whale meat. Other innovations were adopted merely because they filled the place of a vital ingredient. Predominant among these were the dried foods which were imported from the US from 1942 onwards. Four ounces of dried egg equalled nine large eggs and could be used adequately in cakes or as scrambled eggs. Dried meat went direct to restaurants and canteens, but milk, potatoes, and cabbage could all be obtained in dried form for the home. Milk, like eggs, was versatile but the sludgy horror of 'reconstituted potatoes' was one of the lesser wartime burdens.

The herbalist, the vegetarian and the plain crank came into his own. County Herb Committees were formed, under the aegis of the Ministry of Agriculture, to advise what common 'weeds' could be successfully used to eke out the ration. British people for the first time began to experiment with those lethal looking plants which hitherto they had dismissed as 'toadstools', dubiously chewing the spongy tissues of beefsteak fungus and assuring each other that it did, indeed, taste like prime cut steak. Nettles, picked young, tasted like spinach; camomile made a more or less acceptable form of tea. Country-folk inevitably fared better, for not only did they have the wealth of the vegetable kingdom around them but also occasional windfalls of meat from friendly farmers. The slaughtering of animals was supposed to take place under rigorous control — but the accident rate among farm animals soared during the war. 'The poor thing broke its leg, so we put it out of its misery.'

Communal feeding in schools, works' canteens and restaurants eased the burden on the housewife. Food was good, cheap and plentiful in the schools and canteens: a conscript woman factory worker recorded her surprise and delight on sitting down to her midday meal on the first day—a three-course meal, including the traditional meat and two veg, for 1s 2d. The British Restaurants extended the principle to the general population. They were run by the local authorities and were housed in any building that had the space. Spared the necessity of making a profit and with overheads cut to the minimum—the public served themselves—they could afford to sell

canteen, probably at a railway station

meals at less than a shilling a head, inevitably arousing alarm and opposition among the established restaurateurs.

Restaurants were a permanent embarrassment to the Ministry of Food. Again and again the government toyed with the idea of instituting individual rationing for those who used them, so that a person eating an egg in a restaurant would automatically have it docked from his domestic ration. But the insuperable difficulties of administration led to a compromise: meals were to be limited to one main course and a maximum charge of five shillings. The maximum charge was later abandoned for 'superior' restaurants, a loophole which immediately created massive overcharging among the large numbers of restaurants which lay somewhere between Charlie's Caff and the Savoy Grill. In July 1942 the *Spectator* reported that a London restaurant had been heavily fined for charging a cloakroom fee, the 'cloakroom' being a line of pegs in the restaurant itself. 'Fantastic prices are being charged for food. In one restaurant where a house charge of 7s 6d is permitted dinner for two, including some wine—presumably a bottle— came to £2 9s 6d. The maximum charge tends to become a standard charge and many restaurants which used to provide a fixed charge meal at less have put up their price to 5s.' At the other end of the scale the sky was the limit. Sir Henry (Chips) Channon recorded in his diary on one occasion that he had paid £10 at Claridges for lunch for three people.

It is probable that the very poor ate better during the war than at any period before. Feeding the hungry was no longer a charity but part of the 'war effort'. The numbers of school children receiving free or heavily subsidised meals soared: their parents could get balanced meals at proportionately less than they had paid for the bread, marge and fish and chips diet of pre-war years. The vast majority of the population kept good health, were never exactly hungry but were rarely completely satisfied, for there was always some craving that could not be sated. For a tiny minority the war probably made no difference at all. Throughout the war years there was a small but steady trickle of luxury foods—grapes at £1 a bunch, melons at 10s–15s each, wine which, before the war, might have fetched perhaps 5s for a bottle now changing hands at ten times the price. The Black Market in food was never a national problem.

Menu for communal restaurant
in Liverpool

Serving food at a communal feeding centre

There were countless fiddles conducted on a personal basis, but
no organised system to threaten the national system. The most
common source for illegal purchases were the surpluses in
grocers and butchers. In every large town there was a proportion of people who, for one reason or another, did not take up
their ration and it was available to others—at a price.

Certain classes of luxury foods normally sold to such a small
proportion of the population that there was no point in including them in the ration. A correspondent in *Shopping News*
noted: 'The mouth-watering displays of foodstuffs at Fortnum
and Masons this week made me wonder whether rations need
worry anybody. If you're short of anything in the food line I'll
be surprised if you can't get it here.' The diaries of Henry
Channon give no hint of any difficulty in obtaining food,
despite the copious details he gives of domestic arrangements.
On 7 March 1944 he records a dinner party he gave in his home:
'There was gaiety, stimmung, even some drunkenness. The food
was good—oysters, salmon, dressed crab, minced chicken etc. I
counted nineteen cars outside my house. No raid disturbed our
revels and we all wished that Hitler could have seen so luxurious
a festival in London at the height of the war.' The ungenerous
are perhaps tempted to reflect that it would also have been
interesting to have the reaction of the housewife, struggling to
make a meal with a spoonful of dried egg and a couple of carrots, or of the seamen who had brought over the petrol for those

nineteen cars. But, unlike the First World War, such scenes were a minority and it is only fair to add that in the same diaries Channon recounts with admiration how the legendary beauty Lady Diana Cooper plunged enthusiastically into the odorous business of rearing pigs and mucking out byres. The fact that the rich man had his salmon was unimportant: the poor child had his milk.

Early in the rationing period the sausage joined the kipper and mothers-in-law as a standby music-hall joke. Comedians supposed its ingredients to be a state secret, Britain's 'secret weapon' and the like, and the deathless phrase 'breadcrumbs in battledress' neatly summed up the prevailing opinion as to its main ingredient. It also summed up the endless, ingenious attempt to make do and mend as more and more commodities disappeared from the market. Nothing was quite what it seemed, the most unlikely materials were pressed into service to fill a gap. Women were urged to make 'wartime jewellery'— necklaces and earrings of beer-bottle tops, cup-hooks, film spools, corks. The painted woman was now a literal fact for, in the absence of stockings, legs were painted with a variety of commercially produced lotions—some of which had the disconcerting tendency to change colour when exposed to daylight. In their search for cosmetics, some women were tempted to buy the gaudy, very dubious products of the Black Market. Their makers 'know nothing about formulae or hygienic manufacture: they just stir up some sort of mixture on the kitchen stove, cool it, mould it, wrap it up in paper—and hawk it round the shops. Naturally, many shop-keepers refuse to buy these anonymous cosmetics but some, looking round their empty shelves, can't resist the chance of buying a little stock.' One lipstick proved, on analysis, to be virtually crystallised and contained a potentially dangerous admixture of lead. A certain tin of face powder could have been analysed by a layman, for it consisted of nothing but powdered, coloured chalk mixed with a crude scent.

Clothes rationing came into force in June 1941. The results of the delay showed only too clearly what would have happened if food had been left unrationed: clothes prices nearly doubled in a little over eighteen months. Rationing was not by the garment but on a points system: the customer had a maximum number of 'points' and could use them on what article or articles he wished—a system which had been adopted with considerable success for tinned foods and sweets. The financially better-off benefited, for a jacket 'cost' the identical number of points whether it were made in flimsy, but cheap cloth, or of indestructible Harris tweed. But the points system allowed of considerable flexibility for the Board of Trade could stimulate sales of a particular garment by reducing its point value, or check a rush by raising the value. Manual workers were allowed an additional ten coupons per year for working clothes—a fact of which their daughters were only too well aware. Most men appeared to be indifferent—or even welcomed clothes rationing although there was a niggling battle about trouser turn-ups. The Board of Trade forbade them, totting up the thousands of yards of material that would be saved by dispensing with the two-inch turn-up: tailors could be persuaded to add two inches to the length of the trousers for turning up at home. Curiously, the Board did nothing about the length of overcoats. Far greater quantities of material could have been saved by adopting the prestigious knee-length 'British Warm'; instead of which men's coats continued to descend to almost calf length throughout the war.

Men tended to look on their clothing coupons as something to be handled by their womenfolk—or even as beer money: an open trade in clothing coupons developed with coupons changing hands at about 2s 6d each. For women it added an extra dimension to an age-old problem, although the strong probability is that the majority of older women welcomed a release from the tyranny of extreme fashion. George Orwell had expected clothes rationing 'to accentuate class differences, because it is a thoroughly undemocratic measure, hardly affecting well-to-do people who have large stocks of clothes already. However, it now seems "the thing" for people not in uniform to look shabby. The Board of Trade is already contemplating putting everyone into battledress.' That extreme measure was never taken, but women adopted a distinctive wartime dress. The headscarf, once limited to mill girls, became ubiquitous: the shortage of material for hats undoubtedly launched it in society but it maintained its popularity not least because it could cover a multitude of pins in a crisis.

Slacks, before the war, were the badge of the fast woman: now they too came into their own as a warm, decorous garment in any emergency. A variant of the Lancashire clog came into being as the shortage of leather put thick, wooden heels on shoes, bringing the distinctive clacking sound into the streets of the South.

The deceptively-named Utility clothes were at first greeted warily and then welcomed. Anne Scott-James was particularly enthusiastic about them, introducing them to her readers as 'a fashion revolution. They are excellent clothes at government-controlled prices. They cut out luxury and defeat the profiteer. Don't be misled by the term "utility clothes". They have nothing to do with boiler suits and gumboots. They are clothes made from cloth which fulfill certain government refinements and they are sold at fixed prices.' Only two-thirds of all clothing was made to Utility standards and she felt that all clothing should be so controlled, cutting out trimmings and superfluous material which were not only unpatriotic but also in dubious taste. 'If Mayfair hasn't the skill to cut a good dress from three or four yards of material with five or six buttons it must learn—or go under.'

Personal shabbiness was faithfully reflected in the increasing shabbiness of the home. Householders forcibly became aware of the fact that, under normal circumstances, a home was kept going by a continual system of replacement. Again, it was the poorer who suffered most during the earlier months of the war, demonstrating the brutal fact that they possessed fewer items and those of a flimsier quality. But by the middle of the war virtually every household was affected. The supply of new furniture was controlled—but not rationed: the householder could spend only a maximum number of points, but there was no guarantee that the furniture would actually be there to spend it on. Engaged couples could at first claim sixty units to set up house, but this was later cut to thirty, sufficient to buy a bed, table, chairs and perhaps a wardrobe. But if they had the coupons they probably did not have the money. A magazine article in March 1943 strongly advised newly-weds from attempting to set up their own home. 'I'm convinced that it's impossible unless you're a millionaire or something really big on the Black Market to furnish a home today from scratch.' The young seem to have taken the pessimistic advice, for only twelve per cent of newly married couples entered their own home after the wedding: the rest lived with one or other of the parents, exerting additional stresses on the wartime home.

Utility furniture was also introduced in 1942. Miss Scott-James attacked the furniture as vigorously as she had praised the clothes. 'Most of the designs are downright ugly . . . the prices are no cheaper than average second-hand prices and I would consider a well-chosen second-hand chest for £9 a better buy than one for £9 6s 9d.' But the Board of Trade claimed that sixty-five per cent of all customers in furniture shops positively approved of the product. Like Utility clothes, the furniture was limited to specified materials and designs, the buyer having the choice of two qualities and three designs for

Utility furniture introduced in October 1942

each article. The Board engaged the services of top-ranking designers but the products were undoubtedly flimsy to look at, and the speed with which the public abandoned Utility furniture when a wider choice became available after the war argues strongly that customers merely tolerated it out of necessity.

Coloured and fancy crockery disappeared completely from careless households. The craftsmen in the Potteries still pursued their art, but their products were 'for export only', producing badly needed revenue, mostly from the USA. The citizens of the United Kingdom made do with thick, plain white cups — sometimes made without handles. Spoons, when available, were made of an unattractive, light, brittle alloy. Restaurants were particularly vulnerable to the light-fingered and those without pretensions to finesse chained down their spoons. All cutlery was in short supply, for not only was production cut but the vastly expanded Armed Forces took heavy toll of what was available. Most households possessed an adequate collection of knives and forks, but saucepans, which regularly wore out, were at a premium. Long queues would form outside local shops when supplies came in and a woman would count herself lucky to obtain a couple of flimsy saucepans, which would burn out in a matter of months, as the price of an hour's waiting.

Bedding and household linen generally was either unobtainable or for sale at fantastically inflated prices: a Bristol woman complained that she had been asked nine guineas for a pair of single sheets, fifteen guineas for a double pair. Pure luxuries such as bedspreads and tablecloths disappeared from the home, either worn out or transformed into some item of clothing or curtaining. Strictly, there was no need for curtains for the blackout gave total privacy, but few housewives could live with the dreary expanse of blackout curtains. The problem would have been solved for them if the Board of Trade had issued coloured blackout material but the Board was perennially worried that materials intended for one use would be snapped up by the ingenious and used for something quite different. Towels, either white or in an unappetising shade of grey, could occasionally be bought but they were so expensive and of such poor quality that most people preferred to make do with pieces of absorbent cloth.

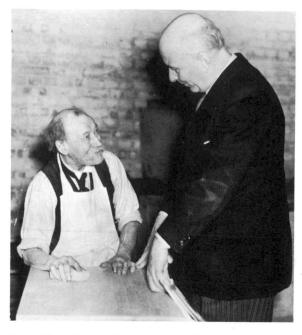

Hugh Dalton, President of the Board of Trade, inspects utility furniture

'Quota' joined the long list of wartime jargon. The shop-keeper was allocated supplies of unrationed goods and when he had sold his current quota of fountain pens, razor blades, toilet paper or whatever he specialised in, he lapsed into a kind of coma until the next allocation. News of the arrival of a quota would spread on an incredibly efficient grapevine and that distinctive wartime phenomenon, the queue, would come into being. It was perfectly possible to create a queue as a practical joke: it needed only two people to stand one behind the other and, sooner or later, a third would join them purely on speculation. It was in the class of non-essential but non-luxury trade that the 'under the counter' system was most widely practised. The wise maintained contacts with shopkeepers over a wide range, calling in frequently and casually, building up a personal acquaintance. A routine developed: if the caller found a stranger in the shop he would pretend elaborate interest in a display, approaching the shopkeeper discreetly afterwards. Then would follow the murmured request and the complaisant nod; there would be a quick glance to ensure that they were unobserved and the article would be slid out from its hiding place and hastily passed over.

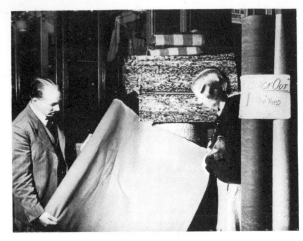

Blackout material, like gas-mask carriers, was a welcome standby for the smaller trader

There is no doubt but that many shopkeepers benefited financially from the business: a man who had been scraping his chin raw with a blunt blade for weeks would pay far above the standard price for a packet of shining new razor blades. But an 'under the counter' transaction was also the product of by no means ignoble motives: the human desire to confer a favour on an acquaintance, the hope of securing a regular customer after the war—above all, the sheer difficulty of survival. In general, the total supply of goods of all kinds was between twenty and thirty-five per cent of the prewar level. Large multiple stores were far better equipped for survival than the small man or specialist, regardless of their relative efficiency, for the departments of large stores carried each other in slack periods. In Glasgow, twenty-five per cent of all small, non-food shops had been forced to close by 1942, an average proportion for all big cities. There was small wonder that a shopkeeper would attempt to make a little hay while the feeble sun shone. But he came in for a large share of obloquy. 'People say, I think with truth, that shopkeepers appear to take a sadistic pleasure in telling you that they don't stock the thing you ask for.' George Orwell noted: 'To go in search of some really rare object such as a comb or a tin of bootpolish is a miserable experience. It means trailing from shop to shop and getting a series of curt or actually hostile negatives. But it is the snubs that they get when they ask for some article which is in short supply that people dread most.' To be fair to the shopkeeper his patience was sorely tried when, hour after hour, he had to give the same answer to the same question and not infrequently be roundly abused for a condition of affairs that was putting him out of business.

Manufacturers of food and domestic goods were faced with a different kind of problem. Some of them were doing vastly better business than before the war by supplying the armed Forces, and scarcely needed the domestic consumer. But the gospel of advertising dictated that they should keep their image before the public gaze. From this consideration arose perhaps the most infuriating series of advertisements. A mouth-watering picture of some luxury food would have as caption 'Not Till After the War' or 'On Active Service', followed by a piece of nostalgic prose. Some manufacturers followed the Ministry of Food's lead and gave hints to their customers as to how to make the most of their products. Lux Toilet Soap ran a useful series on the maintenance and making of clothes; Pyrex oven-ware published recipes—including yet another way to use carrots.

Predictably, some advertisements made crude appeals to patriotism, in particular exploiting the national pride in, and anxiety for 'the troops'. The excruciating doggerel

Now Marigold's become a WAAF
She's writing Goering's epitaph

was tied in tenuously with a brand of biscuit. Tommies marched bravely to war with glittering boots and teeth; Jack Tars gaily sank submarines while sucking jujubes. Noticeably, this type of advertisement tailed off sharply in the middle of the war, the

Once a hat shop, now forced to specialise in the ubiquitous gas mask carrier

reality of death defeating the most dedicated of copywriters. Most advertisements took the line that their product could contribute directly to the war effort. Pet-lovers were urged to give fit and hysteria powders to their dogs when the siren sounded and so reduce the possibility of panic; stick-on soles saved shoe leather; lavatory cleansers reduced the possibilities of disease under war-time conditions. Book publishers faced with sweeping reductions in paper had cause to envy the spaciousness of advertisements. Mr Barratt still took up an entire column to chat to his customers on the virtue of Barratt shoes; Brylcreem occupied a quarter of a column to demonstrate the correct way of shaking the bottle; the ladies queueing for Fry's Cocoa had half a column in which to swap shopping experiences.

The rationing system could not have worked without a back-up system designed to ensure that the regulations were not transgressed. The Ministries concerned called their enforcement officers 'inspectors': the public called them 'snoopers'. The main reason why an organised Black Market in food never came into being was because of the vigilance of the Ministries' huge staff of inspectors and the heavy sentences which could be inflicted in the courts on their evidence. The public applauded when the inspectors unearthed some major transgression of the food regulations; they were less enthusiastic when the inspectors turned their attention to the countless minor breaches which, if left unchecked, would ultimately have wrecked the system. There was small point in the inspector appearing in a shop in the full panoply of office: the whole point of his role was that he should appear to be indistinguishable from any other member of the public. But it was this aspect which particularly exacerbated public opinion and gave birth to the legend of the prowling snooper. Harold Nicolson reported one of these stories in his weekly column in the *Spectator*. It was polished, as all these stories were, down to the last detail and replete with impressive circumstantial evidence. A man, caught in a rainstorm, entered a shop in a small Devon village and asked to buy some socks because his feet were soaked. He had no coupons but promised to send them by post. Moved by his pleading, the shopkeeper parted with the socks, whereupon the customer threw off his mask and revealed himself as an agent of the

Board of Trade. The shopkeeper was reprimanded and fined. Nicolson emphasised that the story was only hearsay, but remarked that he was personally acquainted with a similar case in which an inspector had wheedled a pair of child's slippers from a shopkeeper in exchange for loose coupons.

The stories resulted in a question in the House and a full-scale investigation. The sequel threw a vivid light on the development of rumours. The Parliamentary Secretary to the Board of Trade replied to Nicolson's accusations in a long letter in the *Spectator*. The Devon incident had no basis whatsoever in fact. No village had been traced; no customer with wet feet; no complaining shopkeeper; no court record of any sentence imposed. Turning to the second incident he pointed out that while the story was true in detail it did not cover all the facts: the shopkeeper concerned had been consistently evading the regulations and it was only after four successive inspectors had made illegal purchases that a prosecution was undertaken. The writer pointed out that there was a shortage of experienced staff. 'It is therefore inevitable that on occasions the stringent rules laid down to prevent enticement are not strictly observed. But the cry of "agent provocateur" is apt to become as popular as the latest thriller.'

Further Reading

R. J. Hammond, *Food: Vol I, The Growth of Policy** (1951). E. L. Hargreaves and M. M. Gowing's *Civil Industry and Trade* (1952), gives the general picture of supplies and shortages as they affected civilians. HMSO, *How Britain was Fed in Wartime* (1946). M. M. Postan, *British War Production** (1952).

V

There'll always be an England

On 2 April 1943 the *Spectator* carried an article by a contributor, E. H. M. Relton, who had just returned to England after eighteen months' absence abroad. 'I had imagined, I think, a distinctly shabby lot of people. . . . I was looking for the usual stoic gloom, for apathetic, fatalistic resignation. I saw none of these things. Londoners, far from being shabby, had a clean and prosperous air. The streets and houses were neat. Food was sparse but, to ensure health, adequate. Everybody seemed brisk and purposeful and tough. It compared with the flabbiness that I remembered in pre-war London.'

'Morale' was one of the grossly overworked words of the war. Officialdom spent countless hours in pursuing the almost indefinable, ever-elusive concept: vast sums were set aside to entertain, inform, instruct and assess. It existed: the country, like London was 'brisk, purposeful and tough' but to track the high confidence to its source was to follow the myriad workings of a national character, a dizzying task even though it was made easier by the fact that pressure of war had put a clear, if temporary impress upon a normally amorphous substance.

Religion, the great traditional catalyst, withdrew into the background, playing an uncertain, rather uneasy role. Even as there had been no outburst of xenophobia among the populace generally, so there was no jingoism among the priests of the national Church of the type displayed in the First World War. There was no real crisis of conscience among Christians for this was no dynastic war but a conflict between two ideologies, one of which was demonstrably evil to all but the most determined sophists. Nevertheless, though the steady retreat from organised

94

religion might be temporarily halted by the imminent threat of death, the Churches did not expect to lead, nor did the people expect to be led in the name of religion. The National Days of Prayer were, if anything, an embarrassment with even the devout pondering publicly on the ancient conundrum of God's role when appealed to by conflicting Christians. Here and there the clumsier organs of the State attempted to exploit the machinery of the Church: a clergyman complained that the Ministry of Agriculture had asked him to preach on Digging for Victory, 'enclosing a list of suggested texts with headings on which to base the sermons'. A determined attempt was made to launch a Salvage Day for churches in which congregations were to be exhorted to save every scrap. 'A gentleman connected with the Ministry of Supply preached at St Martins in the Fields last Sunday on a text of his own devising running "Whatsoever a man wastes that shall he lose and he shall lose more than he wastes, and his children's children shall lose after him" —which does not seem an appreciable improvement on the New Testament,' Janus commented in the *Spectator*. He attacked the Church for allowing itself to be used as a publicity medium and later recorded his 'satisfaction and relief' that the Salvage Sunday project is stone dead'.

It was an age of personalities rather than creeds, of political slogans rather than religious dogma. The masses were to be wooed, not pushed and the great descended among them to charm, exhort and encourage. Towering above them was Winston Churchill, elevated by the accident of history from the obscurity of a footnote to the status of a volume. Time has given his dominance an air of inevitability and permanence but contemporary records show that even he was susceptible to the vagaries of democracy. Sir Henry Channon was in regular touch with, and very sensitive to, the mood of the Commons and in his diaries he makes it clear that the Prime Minister's popularity in the House was frequently exactly opposite to what it was in the country. On 23 July 1940 he noted, 'The House is completely with him, as is the country,' but in September, 'The House has become accustomed to his highflown rhetoric and thinks that he jokes too much'. On 17 February 1942 when he addressed the House after the Channel dash of the Scharnhorst and Gneisenau: 'Never have I known

The Prime Minister inspecting House of Commons Home Guard detachment

the House growl at a Prime Minister. Can he ever recover his waning prestige?' After the seizure of Madagascar when he was cheered resoundingly: 'I think he only comes to the House when searching for kudos.' Even the deeply loyal Harold Nicolson noted in 1944 that he was an electoral liability rather than an asset, the Government having just lost two of the rare by-elections to the Common Wealth Party: 'Once the open sea is reached we forget how we clung to the pilot in the storm.' But his extraordinary eloquence, with its daring admixture of resounding phrases and schoolboy slang; his consciously theatrical appearances with the carefully preserved cigar, V-sign and idiomatic costume touched that spring in the people which responded to the positive and the colourful in a confused and dreary world. Looking back at him down the perspective of time A. J. P. Taylor remarked that in 1940 'Churchill was no longer a radical, if he ever had been. He was an eccentric, which exactly suited the mood of the British people.'

Different in kind rather than degree was the response to the monarch. Brought unexpectedly to the throne in the shadow of his glamorous brother, painfully shy and with a severe speech impediment, George VI was not the obvious anointed leader for an embattled country. Politically, he was to remain somewhat out of touch with the current, not least when he wanted to appoint Lord Halifax as Prime Minister after the fall of Neville Chamberlain. Socially, he identified himself totally with his subjects, helped thereto by his own unassuming nature and happy domestic life: the common citizen could see the fears and hopes of his own life exactly reflected in the ultimate stratum of society. The bombing of Buckingham Palace helped to unite monarch and subject more than any other event. It was widely reported how the queen had remarked that she could now 'look the East End in the face'. The fact that the king declined to contemplate leaving the country, or to send his children out of it, when invasion seemed imminent might arguably have led to a difficult situation if a successful invasion had indeed taken place. But it had an incalculable effect upon morale, finally restoring the prestige of the monarchy after its uncertain passage through the 1930s. Less fortunately, the wartime pride in the royal family was to lead directly to the near-hysterical adulation of the early post-war years when the most trivial activities of its members became headline news in certain sections of the Press.

Parliamentary elections were suspended during the war and even by-elections were largely paper transactions. The mass disfranchisement might have led to an increasing gap between

The King and Queen visiting a bombed area

Parliament and people had it not been for the dynamic tension which naturally existed in a government composed of political opposites. The long tenure of office enhanced the personalities of the holders so that ministers who might have been indistinguishable one from the other under normal circumstances emerged into the full light of day. Ernest Bevin, coming from the opposite social pole to Winston Churchill yet curiously resembling him in manner and form, held enormous powers as Minister of Labour. 'He might direct, through his National Service officers, any person in the United Kingdom to perform any service required anywhere.' He was, for most, the epitome of the Labour movement—the practical man who had gained power to do practical things. At the opposite extreme was Stafford Cripps, the pure intellectual, a vegetarian, teetotaller, non-smoker—seemingly totally remote from the commonalty yet, at one period, able to challenge Churchill for the leadership of the country. Both overshadowed Clement Attlee, titular leader of the Party and Churchill's deputy, but the fact that he emerged as a strong prime minister in the chaotic post-war years argues that there was rather more to him than the squeaking mouse of the *Daily Express* cartoon. Herbert Morrison, the perky 'Prime Minister of London', became Home Secretary in the crucial autumn of 1940. Lord Beaverbrook appeared, disappeared and reappeared in the government like some pantomime demon. He brought to the post of

Lord Beaverbrook   *Ernest Bevin*

Minister of Aircraft Production the same flair, the same un-
relenting drive which had characterised his highly successful
newspaper activities. Some of the stunts failed—notably the
aluminium fiasco when millions of housewives donated treasured saucepans to be turned into Spitfires and had the chagrin
of seeing them piled up, unused, because of their low aluminium
content. The concentration of industry on one aspect of war
production caused an imbalance which would have been
dangerous if continued: aircraft were vital—but so were tanks,
rifles, boots, ships. But he ensured a flow of fighter aircraft
during a period when the country's fate hung in the balance.
He became successively Minister of Supply and of War
Production before resigning, on personal grounds, in February
1942.

The national sense of working in common towards a clearly
defined goal gave a touch of glamour even to the dreary business
of financing the war. At one extreme the War Office received a
cheque for £25 from Bitteswell in Leicestershire, the product of
a fifteenth-century fund established 'to find and provide an
armed man out of the village of Bitteswell for the King in time
of war'. At the other extreme were the millions of pounds
collected in the various savings movements. The Spitfire Funds
particularly caught the public imagination. The movement
appears to have started when a colonial newspaper asked the
Minister of Aircraft Production how much a bomber cost to
build: the purely arbitrary figure of £20,000 was given and a
cheque promptly arrived for that amount. But for the general
public the movement was associated with Lady MacRobert of
Dounside. In 1941 she gave a cheque for £20,000 for a bomber
'to carry on the work of her sons' who had been killed in action
with the RAF. The following year she gave another £20,000 for
a flight of four 'MacRobert fighters'. The Spitfire, somewhat
unfairly given the entire credit for the triumph of the Battle of
Britain, was the favourite 'purchase' and all over Britain groups
vied with each other to raise the £5,000 that would 'buy' a
Spitfire to carry their name. 'Money to buy Spitfires has no
more connection with the production of Spitfires than have the
spring flowers,' *The Banker* sourly commented. In cold economic
terms it was perfectly correct but the money was at least withdrawn from circulation and so damped down inflation and it

Member of the WVS
selling war savings
stamps door to door

Savings ceremonial: the Mayor of Islington hands
over 10,000 savings stamps to a representative of
the large local firm which purchased them

gave a sense of participation from the small boy who contributed sixpence for a rivet to the millionaire who 'bought' a flight of bombers.

The National Savings Movement appealed to the cannier elements of the population who preferred to maintain liberty by hire purchase. The Movement was backed by a massive advertising campaign whose expenditure rivalled that of the Ministry of Food. 'Lend to Defend the Right to be Free,' the strident posters exhorted, and the people responded in their millions if for no better reason than that there was little to spend their money on. More than a quarter of a million savings groups came into being—groups in offices, shops, factories, schools and even streets. Each was centred around its collector, the devoted man—or, usually, woman—who every week made the round of the members, extracting the covenanted sixpences or shillings. And at regular intervals the entire community would take part in a week-long 'savings drive', dedicated to one aspect or other of war production—War Weapons Week, Salute the Soldier Week, Warships Week or, the most popular of all, Wings for Victory Week.

The Week became a species of folk ceremony throughout the country. In each locality a target would be set—a few hundred pounds for a village, tens of thousands for a great city—and an indicator set up in some prominent place. On the opening of the Week there was a Grand Parade. In a village the marchers would be drawn largely from the ranks of the Women's Land Army and the wvs, the cadet forces, and the Home Guard with perhaps a detachment from the local anti-aircraft or searchlight site; in the larger cities the parade was a major military affair. The locality which could obtain a piece of enemy equipment— a crashed Messerschmitt fighter was the supreme prize— lugged it along like a Roman triumph. After the parade had passed in review the citizens would be addressed by a local dignitary or, if it was an important city, by a member of the government. Throughout the week that followed there would be a series of concerts, dances, whist drives, military displays, exhibitions of weapons and the like, each with its attendant collectors. And daily the indicator would inch upward, whether the scale was marked in tens or thousands of pounds. The targets set were enormous but were almost invariably passed. Five months after the scheme had been launched, over £160 million had been collected: Liverpool led the list with £11½ million, Heckmondwike claimed the highest amount per head with £42 8s 5d. Fiscally, the value of the Weeks was dubious: the sums which inflated the enormous totals tended to be the millions of the established financial companies rather than the shillings of the private citizen. But 'they are the answer to the cry, voiced at various times and by various people from Winston Churchill to J. B. Priestley that there should be more flag waving, more music and more colour and pageantry to this business of winning the war', *Picture Post* claimed.

The unregenerate continued to spend their money on frivolities, undeterred by the ferocious Squanderbug whose portrait, with the legend 'Wanted for Sabotage', snarled from countless hoardings. The Squanderbug was the child of the National Savings Movement: his frivolous counterpart, Mr Chad, was the child of the people. The long-nosed face peering over a wall, with its wisp of hair in the shape of a question mark and its mocking query 'Wot—no fags?'—or biscuits or beer or whatever, was the demotic reply to the high-minded exhortations. Millions read the Trappist plea of the National Savings Committee to 'Buy nothing for your personal pleasure or comfort, call on no labour' on their way to dog track or pub or cinema. Taxation took increasing bites out of their income, but wages too had risen—by as much as eighty per cent on the 1938 level—and in the absence of durable goods to spend the money on, people turned increasingly to entertainment. The Churches' Committee on Gambling reported that tote gambling alone on ninety-two dog tracks had increased from £36 million in 1938 to £42 million in 1942. Attendance at football matches slumped, partly from the wholesome fear of being caught in a crowd of thousands in a raid, partly from the fact that star players, such as Stanley Matthews, were serving with the Forces. But the pools went on. The promoters were an easily identified target for the moralists and they did what they could to forestall criticism, banding together into a single Unity Pool to save staff and overheads and publishing their coupons in newspapers instead of overloading the attentuated mail service. 'Doing the pools' was as good a way as any of passing a tedious evening and there was still a chance of winning thousands for a penny.

Public houses were badly affected during the period of heavy raids. Again there was a reluctance to be unnecessarily caught in a crowd and a rumour arose, too, that pubs were specific targets for the bombers—presumably because of their traditionally conspicuous nature. But after the raids pub-going soared. People who, before the war, would never have dreamt of setting foot in such an establishment now found themselves part of a group, whether in Forces or factory or warden's post, who had no such inhibitions. The pub, too, presented an oasis of light and warmth and good fellowship in a blacked out, hostile world. One of the causes of the decline in drunkenness despite the increase in pub attendance was that the beer was heavily watered and spirits virtually unobtainable. Imports of foreign spirits were cut to almost nothing and Scotland's great gift to civilisation was now reserved mostly for the American market, earning vital dollars. Public houses, too, had their quota. 'Sorry, no beer' joined the dismal list of notices and the respectable thirsty had no choice but to join the reprehensible pub-crawl in order to obtain perhaps two half-pints of weak

Poster designed by 14-year-old girl for school savings campaign

War-time pub: the London Wine Bar in Lime Street, Liverpool

beer after half-a-dozen visits. The shortage left a permanent
mark on drinking habits: the great quart mug finally disappeared and the half-pint took its place beside the pint as
a socially acceptable measure.

'Is your journey really necessary?' the posters demanded of
the traveller as he approached a railway station. The answer
would seem to be an unqualified yes. The station master at
Kettering commented: 'We pack people in as if they were
cattle and they do not seem to mind. There was a case recently
when a woman was taken ill and died on a train and before she
could be got out of the compartment ninety-five people had to
be asked to get off the train.' Every major shortage affected the
railways—coal, staff, steel, food—and their total services were
cut by more than a third. But simultaneously official demand
soared: entire passenger trains were taken over for troop movements and those that remained in the civilian service had their
heavy quota of servicemen and women proceeding inde-
pendently on leave. War-workers, directed perhaps hundreds

of miles from their homes, swelled the total as they commuted for hours to snatch a day at home. In addition to the misery of overcrowding and the inevitable squalor that it produced was the sheer tediousness of the journeys. A bomb on the line or a priority shipment could delay scores of trains. During the period of heavy raids even an alert in the vicinity meant that the train had to stop at the next station for passengers to seek shelter if they wanted and speed was reduced to about 20 mph. Journeys across Britain took on the status of continental crossings: one woman took two days to travel from Norwich to Glasgow. Commuters from the thirty-mile ring around London could spend almost as long in travel as they spent in work. After dark, travellers were denied even the relief of reading: trains were not blacked out and only the dimmest of lights could therefore be provided in trains without blinds or curtains. Food, once simply a means of whiling away a journey, became as rare as a vacant seat. A few restaurant cars ran until surprisingly late in the war, but most people were forced to rely on the grossly overcrowded station buffets with their plethora of 'Sorry, no—' notices, their chained spoons, cracked cups and curious liquids indifferently passing as tea or coffee. Members of the Forces were somewhat better served. Most stations had their canteens, staffed at ungodly hours by devoted bands of middle-aged women, and serving a range of food that was limited, but was

Daylight raid on a station at peak hour: a single bomb caused this damage

Commuters finish their journey on foot due to bomb on line 1940

certainly more wholesome than that in the public buffets.

Nevertheless, despite—or, probably because of—the appalling conditions there was a spirit of shipboard camaraderie. 'The making of friends had never been so easy,' H. E. Bates noted. 'In the whole history of British railways there has never been, I should think, so much conversation and friendliness per mile as now. The air of silent refrigeration, the arid cross-examination of stares, the snoozing behind the fat peacetime blankets of newspapers—all that has gone. It has never been so easy to get all kinds of people to talk of themselves.'

The symbol of the camaraderie of the roads was the jerked thumb and ingratiating look of the hitch-hiker. Almost unknown before the war, hitch-hiking was now not only made respectable by custom but also recommended by law: a single occupant of a car was likely to be stopped by the police who were empowered to ask some pretty searching questions as to the source of the petrol and the reasons for the journey. The supply of petrol to the private motorist was cut off in stages: until 1942 it was possible to drive for about 150 miles a month but in the March of that year the 'basic ration' was abolished altogether. Morality as well as economics was responsible for the removal of the non-essential private car from the road. The peculiar dangers that the men of the tanker fleets ran to bring petrol to Britain made an enormous impact on the popular imagination and the spectacle of thousands of cars at race meetings, in particular, aroused fierce indignation. After the abolition of the basic ration, private motorists could claim a supply only if it were essential for work or health. People, such as farmers, who could claim a commercial as well as a personal ration, had to distinguish very clearly between one use of petrol and another. Commercial petrol was died red, and if the police found traces of red in the engine of a non-commercial vehicle the owner could be heavily fined. Inevitably, a black market came into being, for it was comparatively simple to remove the red dye, but the heavy penalties for the misuse of petrol—penalties which included imprisonment—deterred all but the most fanatical of automaniacs. In the early period of rationing experiments were made with gas as a means of propulsion. Ordinary town gas could drive a converted engine and cars appeared on the road with enormous, billowing bags strapped to the roof—and catching every gust of wind. But refuelling was needed every ten miles or so and when fuel shortage affected the supply of gas, the experiment was abandoned. Gas generators, towed on a trailer, lasted a little longer but for most private motorists their maintenance was far more trouble than they were worth, and by the end of 1942 the

The first of the short-lived town gas supply stations: March 1940

vast majority of private cars were laid up 'for the duration'.

But car-owning was still, in any case, the luxury of a minority; it was the curtailment of the bus services which affected more people, in particular in rural areas. Buses suffered all the shortages which affected the railways, with the addition of the tyranny of the black-out. Perhaps the most nerve-wracking civilian job of the war was to be the driver of a double-decker, grossly overcrowded with passengers, inching his vehicle through darkened but populated streets. On country routes, all points of reference disappeared after dark and a driver new to a route could only too easily end up in a field, particularly at a curve. Outside the big cities, bus services stopped at 9 p.m. and even in London the last buses ran long before 11 p.m. More and more people took to bicycles, but these, pleasant and safe enough in daytime, were lethal in the big cities after dark. Some civilians could cadge lifts on the army lorries which took servicemen out of the towns to their camps after nightfall, but for the majority social life, perforce, ended early unless they had complaisant hosts. George Orwell noted that 'it is becoming a common practice when you dine at anybody else's house to sleep there'.

The 'Holidays-at-Home' movement was specifically intended to damp down demand for travelling, but its benefits rubbed off on to the very large proportion of the population who, in the past, could not have afforded to go away in any case. The organisation was at municipal level, and the London boroughs were particularly imaginative with comedians in Russell Square, drama on Clapham Common, village-type carnivals in Hyde Park. The British, who traditionally viewed with deep suspicion the foreign habit of enjoying themselves in the open, now found themselves eating, drinking and even dancing in the parks and squares and public gardens of the country. The newspapers and magazines loyally plugged the attractions of boating on the Thames, picnicking on Wimbledon Common, exploring Epping Forest and the like. Viewed in the right spirit it was even possible to make an attraction out of a deck chair, a newspaper and a pot of tea in the back garden.

Holiday camps for war-workers were organised by a joint committee from the Ministry of Labour and local authorities. At Cookham in Berkshire the war-worker could enjoy a week-

*ENSA : adaptation of the
classical chorus line*

end for 7s 6d or a whole week for 30s, sleeping communally in
wooden huts, eating communally in the open air—a Spartan
but gregarious life which apparently had its own attractions for
it was never short of applicants. A more sybaritic life was
offered by the camps established in stately homes generously
loaned by their owners. The food was the same, but it was at
least possible to enjoy Spam and chips, or cauliflower cheese,
in an Inigo Jones dining room.

Official entertainment and recreation was, altogether,
organised on the biggest scale since the days of Imperial Rome.
J. B. Priestley told his *Postscript* listeners of one incident that
stuck in his mind. 'The other day I saw two thousand people
push aside what remained of the meat pies and fried plaice and
chips they'd had for lunch, lift their eyes towards an orchestra
consisting of four young women in green silk and then, all two
thousand of them, roar out "Oh Johnny, O, Johnny how you
can love". And having paid this tribute to Johnny and applauded the four young women in green silk these two thousand
people returned, much heartened, to another five or six hours
work at their machines.'

The place was a factory and the orchestra was provided by
ENSA, an organisation which undoubtedly brought more
pleasure to more people and attracted more abuse than any
other organisation in theatrical history. The *Daily Telegraph*
carried the deadpan report that 'ENSA describes as without
foundation an allegation by an actor that members of the

Forces have had to be locked in at its performances'. The more independent comedians it employed found in it a fruitful source for gags. But the attacks upon it were, if anything, an index of its success: the demand for ENSA programmes vastly outstripped the supply of first-rate, or even competent theatrical talent. Entertainments National Service Association was the creation of the theatrical producer Basil Dean whose triumph was to evolve a national organisation out of a traditionally anarchic profession while yet keeping a sharp eye on the standards of individual performers. Fees were low, but the attraction of a regular salary, and the exemption from call-up, undoubtedly brought in large numbers of 'artistes' who would have been better employed in almost any other capacity. Comedians with a limited fund of filthy stories, ageing soubrettes with the desperate smiles born of countless windy pier-ends, tap dancers who fell over, jugglers who dropped their baubles, cat-trainers whose cats ignored them, imitators who rendered even Churchill unrecognisable — these and others like them appeared far too often on far too many stages. Dean rooted them out ruthlessly when they caught his attention but the many who got through gave ENSA its distinctive flavour. But on the credit side were the hundreds of competent people who made long journeys to visit some remote camp site, or endured the clatter of knives and forks at works canteens to bring a brief touch of colour and glamour to a grey working day for a wage of around £8 per week.

The long dominance of London as the cultural centre was temporarily diminished: British citizens in even remote villages now had the chance to enjoy performances hitherto limited to the West End. The Yorkshire mining village of Askern asked Jack Jackson's May Fair Band to come and play in the village. Somewhat to the committee's astonishment, the band agreed. 'The four bob tickets (regrettably) changed hands at ten, fifteen, even twenty shillings,' but Askern created its own small record as 'the first mining village to dance to a West End band'. Sadlers Wells, bombed out in London, went out on a lengthy tour of the provinces; so, too, did the Ballet Rambert and the Old Vic. CEMA — the Council for Education in Music and the Arts — originated these tours as well as a variety of travelling exhibitions and chamber concerts. But just as ENSA was attacked for its low standard so, predictably, CEMA was castigated for being 'highbrow'. The *Daily Express* donned its John Bull hat and machine-gun prose to attack it.

The government gives £50,000 to help wartime culture. What sort of madness is this?

There is no such thing as culture in wartime.

But thousands disagreed, paying their sixpences to hear Myra Hess in the National Gallery, their shillings to listen to Sybil Thorndike in the draughty hall of some Welsh mining town, queuing up for the Proms under Malcolm Sargent in the Albert Hall—but also filling canteens to hear an obscure quartet.

The song-writers had greeted the outbreak of war with a turgid flood of patriotic numbers: twenty-seven emanated from seven publishers alone in the first three months. Their themes were divided between the sentimental and the bellicose. What was begun in 1914–18 was to be finished now:

> *Here we go again,*
> *Up the line again,*
> *But this time its gonna be the last time*

The German leaders were the target for remarkably puerile insult:

> *Heil Hitler, yah, yah yah,*
> *O what a horrid little man you are*

The most embarrassing of all was undoubtedly *We're gonna hang out the washing on the Siegfried Line*. When it first appeared it was supposed to have caused great offence in Germany and the German propagandists certainly produced their own version in retaliation:

> *We're gonna cry out stinking fish until the end of time*
> *Have you any stinking fish Britannia dear?*

But the Siegfried Line remained as quiet as a country lane and when the Allied Armies were hurled many hundreds of miles from it the song was discreetly dropped from the repertoire.

Most of the numbers produced in the first months of the war died a natural death, their cash-engendered patriotism proving unequal to reality. But the song that was virtually to become the unofficial national anthem was written, for a film, shortly before war broke out. *There'll always be an England* was patriotism pure, undefiled and mindless in which England's possession of country lanes and cottages small made it unique among nations. The tune was rousing but the words would have created a gooseflesh of embarrassment under normal conditions. But the English, who habitually mumbled their national anthem in a shamefaced manner, roared and thumped

> *Red White and Blue*
> *What does it mean to you?*
> *Surely you're proud,*
> *Shout it aloud.*

as though they were unstable Continentals.

The German propagandists who claimed that the Siegfried Line song was not written by soldiers 'because soldiers do not brag' were accurate enough. 'The troops' ungratefully ignored the bellicose offerings of the professional songwriters and evolved or adopted their own choice of lyrics, most of them ironic or irrelevant to the war. The Royal Navy marked the appalling tragedy of the *Hood* in a seemingly callous refrain

> *Roll on the Rodney, the Nelson, Renown,*
> *They can't sink the 'Ood 'cause the 'Ood 'as gone down.*

ENSA : factory concert. The lone entertainer is wearing the ENSA 'uniform' of dark blazer and light trousers

The Army perversely borrowed an enemy lyric and gave *Lili Marlene* to the British public. The RAF contributed the mocking *Bless 'Em All* and launched *Roll Out the Barrell*, the song nearest to the universal appeal of *Tipperary* that the Second World War was to produce.

It was probably also in air-crew messes that the gnomic *Green grow the rushes O* was revived. The newest of the three services had the widest effect on popular habits and speech. The Army was designed to serve abroad: the Navy was confined to coastal areas, but the RAF was distributed throughout the population. Both its offensive and defensive roles were immediately obvious to every civilian: gratitude for the fighters of the Battle of Britain was succeeded by a sense of participation in the bombing raids of the later period. The great victories in the Western Desert were something for national pride, but the knowledge that Berlin was being pounded had a personal significance for those who had endured the Blitz. RAF slang permeated civilian speech. David Langdon summed it up neatly in the caption to a cartoon of two civil servants, one saying to the other 'Give me a buzz on the intercom at eleven hundred hours and we'll bale out for coffee'. Office boys complained how the boss had 'shot them down in flames' for a misdemeanour. People 'took a pretty poor view' of an unfavourable situation, 'tore somebody off a strip' for a careless piece of work, described an easy task as 'a piece of cake', pronounced such and such a thing to be 'wizard' or 'ropey'. They 'stooged around' to fill in time, 'pranged' through carelessness and declared themselves 'browned off' with the war, with rationing, with any tedious situation. They adopted the aircrew's gremlin as universal scapegoat for anything that went wrong. The little creature—part gnome, part elf, part goblin—was perhaps the last popular revival of the supernatural. Some aircrews really did seem to believe that a malicious entity was tampering with their aircraft, usually in flight, and though its activities were invariably discussed jocularly, it was with an undercurrent of unease. The name passed into popular speech and was given a varied etymology, ranging from an amalgam of *G*raham's Lager and *F*remlin's Beer to a scholarly derivation from the OE verb *greme*—to vex.

In common with all other places of public entertainment,

ENSA : concert for shelterers in Aldwych underground station. The audience is sitting on the railway track which has been specially boarded over for the occasion

theatres were closed on the outbreak of war. The panic measure was eased during the autumn of 1939 and by the time of the Fall of France the theatre was back to a semblance of normality. Then, hardly believing the evidence of their own box offices the theatre managers watched the tide of playgoers swell to a flood. A boom was in being. The boom was short-lived, the Blitz putting a clear-cut end to it but while it lasted even plays that would have mercifully disappeared after a trial run played night after night to packed houses. Thereafter, the popularity of the theatre coincided with the ebb and flow of war. In the winter of 1941 'the few whose need of entertainment took them abroad after dark found only the little Windmill open, gallantly living up to its label—non-stop revue—in an unexpectedly literal sense'. The courageous, scantily clad young girls became, for the Second World War, what their mothers had been in *Chu Chin Chow* in the First. The company slept on the premises and night after night, whatever was happening in the skies overhead, the Revue made its gaudy, fragile, indestructible gesture of defiance. It was an impressive and, ultimately, legendary example of the human capacity to maintain routine under the most violent conditions of abnormality. After the war the management, justly proud, used the laconic phrase 'We never closed' as its most potent advertisement and the little theatre became one of the fixed points of tourist London.

The second theatrical boom also coincided with a major military event—this time, the German attack on Russia in the June of 1941. It is curious why the theatre, alone among entertainments, should have been immediately affected by such external causes. Certainly there was little in its performances to act as a patriotic catalyst. At the lowest level patriotism was, predictably, expressed by dressing chorus girls in Britannia's shield and helmet and draping them in Union Jacks. At the 'serious' level the war found little expression. The *Annual Register*, discussing Cronin's play, *Jupiter Laughs*—in which a doctor is converted from cynicism by the death of the girl he loves—observed that, though it was a failure, 'it proved to the discerning that London was not, as it had been in the last war, wholly given over to escapism and frivolity'. Nevertheless, the vast majority of the successful productions were comedies. Noel Coward's *Blithe Spirit*—barracked by outraged Spiritualists on its opening night—was unrepentantly escapist with its tale of ghosts and mediums in a middle-class Never-Never land. Terence Rattigan's *While the Sun Shines* recognised the war but used it simply as providing the machinery for farce. Later, his *Flarepath* did provide a serious comment on the war for contemporaries and, for posterity, a poignant recreation of one segment of it—how the wives of bomber crews reacted to their husbands' razor-edge balance between two contrasting worlds. But it was the classic revivals which dominated the serious stage: Shakespeare in particular, embodying as he did the national fears and hopes in the historical plays, enjoyed an immense popularity. Phrases which, for thousands, had been embedded in battered, ink-stained school texts, now took on a new and thrilling significance. One of the most fortunate theatrical coincidences of all time was the release of the filmed *Henry V* at the very end of the European war.

If the ancient world of the stage was unable to fulfil its traditional role, the brand new world of electronics more than adequately filled the gap. Playgoing was, increasingly, a minority experience: the better singers and comedians in particular were increasingly exchanging the uncertainty of the boards for the regularity of the microphone. Some tried, with varying degrees of success, simply to transfer their stage persona and patter to the BBC studio. But the distinctive radio show of the war was the comedy series loosely built around one or two stars in a series of flexible situations. It originated in America and first appeared in Britain when *Bandwagon*, with Arthur Askey and Richard Murdoch, went on the air on 16 September 1939. The immensely popular *Gang Show* was built around two American stars, Bebe Daniels and Ben Lyon. Their arrival in Britain was headline news. 'Bebe and Ben are back again. They have been held up in Lisbon and were rescued by the Ministry of Information which issued a special pass enabling them to catch a plane and prevent millions of listeners from being disappointed.' Not all the readers of that item were enchanted by the news: Douglas Reed, for one, sourly contrasted the BBC's obeisance to mid-Atlantic culture with its cavalier treatment of Britain's own heritage. But the public thought otherwise, relishing the quick-fire wisecracks which it had been taught to associate with fashionable American humour.

The coinciding of an artiste, a period and a medium produced the unique *Itma*. Radio was the ideal—indeed, the only possible medium—for its fantasy world. At the height of its popularity a film was made of it, but this was a resounding flop, the surrealist characters of the radio show emerging as stock comic figures on film. It might possibly have developed a peacetime personality as compelling as that evolved during the war but, judging by the fate of other popular wartime shows, this seems unlikely. It certainly did not survive the death of its anchor man, Tommy Handley, in 1949. The programme first appeared just before war broke out and its title—*It's that Man Again*—was the last jaunty reference to the peacetime view of Hitler: later, it was applied to Handley himself. Handley became a national institution, accorded the ultimate honour of a memorial service in St Paul's, but the success of *Itma* was the indivisible product of a team—in particular that of the script writer, Ted Kavanagh, the producer Francis Worsely and the mimic Jack Train. Handley appeared variously as the Minister of Aggravation and Mysteries in the Office of Twerps, the Mayor of Foaming at the Mouth and such-like improbable

public figures. The plot was minimal: with Handley as the constant centre, keeping up an incredibly rapid fire of jokes, comments and appalling puns, a succession of weird characters, each identified with its catchline, contributed their quota to the crazy world. Some of the characters were ousted by later arrivals: Funf, the German spy, appeared in the earlier months as a reflection of the prevailing spy-mania but later sank to a minor role. Others appeared in every performance, regardless of the supposed requirements of plot: Colonel Chin-strap, the bibulous survivor of Mafeking; Signor So-So, the Italian carpet seller; Mrs Mopp, whose name was to enter the language along with Sairey Gamp's; the melancholy Diver, as inconsequential as a character in *Alice in Wonderland*; the ex-gangster Lefty with his compulsive machine-gunning. A very large proportion of the available time was taken up by their catch-phrases, each awaited eagerly by the audience, greeted with a burst of laughter, and afterwards used again and again in common speech. A fighter pilot baling out was heard to use the Diver's plaintive phrase 'I'm going down now, sir': Mrs Mopp's 'Can I do you now sir?', So-So's 'No likey? Oh, Crikey', Chinstrap's 'I don't mind if I do'—these and a score of others were so woven into the vernacular that it seemed remarkable that the English could ever have communicated before *Itma* was invented. The programme owed much of its attraction to its topicality. When the capture of the Russian town of Veliki Veluki was announced on the six o'clock news, Signor So-So that same evening varied his ritual praise of his wares with the phrase

The cast of Much Binding in the Marsh *including (l. to r.) Kenneth Horne, Sam Costa, Richard Murdoch*

'Very veliki, very veluki' and the esoteric name passed into English speech for a brief period. This widespread, automatic use of the catchphrase was doubtless childish but it was also, perhaps, an unconscious affirmation of national unity: there were no longer mutually exclusive groups each with its jargon but one vast group sharing even flippant clichés in common.

Itma celebrated the embattled civilian; significantly, the only successful programme to do the same for the services was *Much Binding in the Marsh*, chronicling the life of a very mythical RAF station. There were only three major characters, the pompous AOC played by Kenneth Horne, Richard Murdoch's bumbling Adjutant and the mutinous, all-purpose, perpetually 'binding' airman, played by Sam Costa. There were no catchphrases, though the jaunty little theme song was capable of seemingly infinite adaptation, but it exploited the possibilities of radio perhaps even more than did *Itma*, creating an enclosed little world of its own. The last wartime programme, in which the three men walked through the empty, echoing hangars and offices to bid farewell to the station's sole aircraft, the Cabbage White MK IV, achieved a curious degree of reality and poignancy, foreshadowing the nostalgia for the war that was to be so marked a feature in the first postwar generation.

Further Reading
Mass Observation, *War begins at home*, contains a highly evocative account of popular songs in the first months of war. Basil Dean, *The Theatre at War* (1956), for the development of ENSA. Guy Morgan, *Red Roses Every Night: an account of London Cinema's under fire*. For the *Itma* story: Francis Worsley, *ITMA 1939–1948* (1948).

VI

Go To It

In September 1939 there were one and a quarter million unemployed in the United Kingdom: after six months of total war
the number had actually risen, despite the existence of the
National Services (Armed Forces) Act which made liable for
conscription every able-bodied male between the ages of
eighteen and forty-one. The hard core of the unemployed was
formed of the last victims of the Depression but their numbers
were inflated by the victims of a war which had not yet begun
to be fought. There was little point in building houses which
would infallibly be destroyed, so some 200,000 building
workers were sacked, to be followed by a similar number of
shop assistants and allied workers. The entertainment industries contributed their quota: usherettes from the closed
cinemas and theatres, attendants from thousands of seaside

April 26, 1939 : the first conscripts were liable only to six months service

amusement arcades, itinerant ice-cream salesmen, deck-chair attendants, chorus girls—all those who worked in the fringe world outside the office and the factory.

In the spring of 1940 the war machine gradually, but still slowly, began to pump dry this enormous reservoir of labour. Conscription for the Armed Forces took the biggest single gulp. The introduction of conscription even before the war, and the creation of the 'Reserved occupations' list, gave the clearest possible indication to the British public that this war was to be different in kind from the last. There was no place for the generous, but economically unbalancing impulse of the volunteer in an industrial society whose parts increasingly interlocked one with the other. Registration for conscription proceeded by age-groups, beginning with the youngest. On registering, the man declared the nature of his present employment: if it was listed as a reserved occupation, he was automatically excluded from conscription for the forces. The list was flexible: a key worker in a vital industry received total exemption—although, under the increasing demands for manpower such exemptions were put through ever finer sieves; others, including apprentices and students, could receive deferment from time to time. By the time conscription was in full swing it was morally certain that any man in civilian clothes had justified himself to a cold official scrutiny. As a result, the hysterical 'white feather' movement of the previous war, when patriotic beldames pressed the coward's symbol even into the hands of soldiers on leave, never took hold. Conscripted men perhaps displayed a wry envy of their more fortunate colleagues, and uniformed camaraderie led to an amiable contempt of Civvies but there was, in general, a vivid awareness that the serviceman was a citizen in uniform and the civilian—particularly the civilian in the Blitz—was perforce another kind of fighter. The list of reserved occupations made explicit what was implicit: in cold military terms the man who made the gun was as vital as the man who fired it.

The conscript was still allowed, in theory, to choose which of the three Armed Forces he wished to serve in. The Royal Navy was still first choice and it was probably the only one among the auxiliary and regular services to be manned wholly by volunteers. But it was also the smallest of the services: its manpower

September 4, 1939: the 'Call-up'

at the maximum period was 783,000 men, compared with the million men in the RAF in March 1944 and the 2,920,000 men in the army at the end of the war. The RAF was second choice both among young bachelors, attracted by the glamour of the air-crew, and among family men who reasoned that an RAF posting was likely to be conveniently near home. The army seemed to possess few attractions for anybody, but its overwhelming demand for men ensured that the majority of would-be sailors and airmen ended up carrying a rifle. A boy over the age of fourteen could marginally increase his chances of entering a desired service by joining one of the cadet forces—the Sea Cadet Corps, the Air Training Corps, or the Army Cadet Force—and volunteering shortly before his eighteenth birthday. If he had learned the rudiments of a trade—signalling, in particular—and there was a shortage of such tradesmen in his preferred service at the time of volunteering, he was accepted.

The allocation of leave varied greatly and completely arbitrarily, faithfully reflecting the official opinion that 'leave' was a privilege to be granted or withheld at official discretion. At one extreme there was the serviceman drafted to the Far East who could expect to remain there for years on end: at the other extreme was the stores clerk at a local depot who could hope to spend each night in his bed. Differing conditions of service necessarily affected frequency and duration of leave even among servicemen stationed in the same area. The seaman, absent on patrols lasting three weeks or even more, was in an obviously very different position from the airman whose operational sortie was measured in hours but, on average, servicemen in the United Kingdom could reasonably expect about one week's leave in every three months. Travel warrants were issued for these longer leaves but for the shorter twenty-four or forty-eight hour passes the serviceman usually had to make his way home at his own expense, a fact which explained the prevalence of hitch-hiking as a means of wartime transport.

Arguably, it was the two and a half million wives of service-men who bore the heaviest burden of the war, for they were not only denied their husband's support during the rigours and terrors of war but were also financially penalised for doing so. Despite the social changes over the past generation it was still assumed that the man who actually fought for his country should be paid at a far lower rate than the man who made the weapons. The war-worker could earn £1 a day or even more: the private soldier was paid 3s a day. Until the very last year of the war a grateful government paid his wife 25s a week—and stopped 7s a week from his pay for the purpose. In 1944 the allowance was raised to £3 a week for a wife with two children. The existence of food subsidies, and the provision of cheap or free welfare foods and meals ensured that the serviceman's family was protected from actual want, from actual starvation. But if his wife wanted to enjoy a standard of living which at least approximated that of the war-worker's wife she had little alternative but to go out to work, whatever the psychological effect it might have upon her children.

The conscription of males for military service is probably as old as civilisation itself: the conscription of men—and women—for civilian labour was unprecedented in a democracy. But, inevitably, it came, the obverse side of the argument that the man who made the gun was as vital as the man who fired it. Throughout 1940 the demands for manpower increased— from the Armed Forces, from the Civil Defence Services and from the war factories. Simultaneously, demands came from industries not immediately connected with the war effort but obviously vital for its pursuance. Farmers, in particular, were not only struggling to run their farms with a depleted labour force but were being urged to plough ever more acres and so reduce the total of food imports. 'Manpower' was as much a munition of war as was coal or steel or money and to continue the present system of piecemeal supply and demand was to court disaster. In the autumn of 1940 a systematic review of the situation was made, and at the end of the year a new phrase came into being—the 'manpower budget'. In the words of the official historians the budget 'was the only method the War Cabinet ever possessed of determining the balance of the whole war economy by a central and direct allocation of physical resources among the various sectors . . . the main force in determining every part of the war effort from the number of RAF heavy bombers raiding Germany to the size of the clothing ration.' The gaps now became clearer and, to fill them, conscription was extended: all men between the ages of eighteen and fifty-one were obliged to register for National Service— and so were all unmarried women between the ages of twenty and thirty. The list of reserved occupations disappeared: each case was now judged on its merit. The Essential Works Order could move a worker from one part of the country to another, or force him to stay where he was.

The unprecedented conscription of women predictably caused a furore, particularly when, in 1943, the age-range was extended upwards to fifty-one. But it was the logical conclusion of a process which had begun in the previous war when women had first emerged from the shelter of the home to work side by side with men. Domestic responsibilities alone were not enough to ensure exemption: the woman had to be able to prove if necessary that her children were still dependent upon her or

Member of the WRNS arriving at barracks

that her husband's war-work would be adversely affected by her absence. But, on the whole, it was the unmarried woman in her twenties who was most likely to be affected. About a quarter of all 'mobile' women—some 460,000—chose one or other of the women's auxiliary services. The Wrens—the Women's Royal Naval Service—again proved first choice: peacetime memories of yachting probably contributed to the belief that it was socially superior to its sister services. The popularity of the other two services were the reverse of their male equivalents, possibly because the ATS uniform was undeniably smarter than that of the WAAF's or because it was the only service in which men and women worked together in action. The ATS crew working on AA gun sites and searchlight batteries were the nearest the country was to see of the Amazon armies predicted by the objectors to women's conscription. Most women in the auxiliaries were employed on clerical and kitchen duties, although WRNS crews manned small boats in ports and the ATS or WAAF chauffeur was one of the perks of reasonably high armchair office.

The destination of a large proportion of conscripted women was one of the great Royal Ordnance Factories, via a Government Training Centre which also gave an elementary training to the thousands of men who had been directed from non-essential jobs. Popular newspaper and magazine articles of the period gave the impression that factory life was one long sing-song and round of ENSA entertainment, interspersed with visits to the factory hairdresser and masseur. But though it came as a shock to thousands of women to learn that people did indeed work long hours in noise and draughts and dirt, most adapted well to an alien type of life. Shopgirls and domestic servants, in particular, found the free and easy relationship, and the sense of being engaged on productive work a refreshing contrast to their normal work. The skilled craftsmen treated the advent of this painted, scented, manicured work-force with a mixture of mockery and suspicion that later changed to respect and then a matter-of-fact acceptance. As one of the girls told a reporter, 'At first you think you'll never do it. You drop your tools and everything. But the men are very good. They teach you.' Ultimately, it would have been impossible to force any woman to remain in a factory against her will: in theory she could be

Aircraft factory: rolling out
metal bands during construction
of bomber

Aircraft factory: the 'dope shop'

fined or even imprisoned for defying direction but a mutinous, deliberately careless woman on a production team would have defeated the whole object of her enforced presence. The incompatible weeded themselves out: they could be directed again but usually into employment that was personally more congenial to them. The vast majority who remained treated it like any other job which would augment the housekeeping.

The long working day—sometimes extending for as much as eleven hours and averaging fifty-five hours over the week— inevitably produced absenteeism. Most women started work before the shops opened and finished long after they were closed and had little alternative but to take off unofficial time in order to do the family shopping. In theory, habitual absenteeism was also punishable by law but, in practice, the numbers involved were far too great for the law to have effect. Mass resistance also defeated the well-meaning campaign to persuade women to change their hairstyle. The Veronica Lake 'bang'—a heavy tress of hair falling negligently over the face—caused the scalping of many an unfortunate as the hair was caught up in a moving machine. American factories were faced with a similar problem and the actress patriotically put her hair up for the duration, but the style continued in modified form, despite the warning posters.

Outside the factories, the most obvious areas affected by the feminine invasion was in transport and on the land. 'Clippies' almost entirely replaced the male bus conductors and on the Underground and at mainline stations women guards, ticket-collectors and even porters appeared. A grateful nation praised their efforts and continued to pay them at rates far below that of their male colleagues.

Agriculture created one of the major demands for female labour and ultimately some 90,000 women between the age of eighteen and forty were enrolled in the Women's Land Army. The war benefited farming more than any other industry: it could hardly have done otherwise, considering the abysmal state to which it had sunk between the wars. The large promises made to farmers during the food crisis of 1917–18 had been forgotten during the following boom and slump. Despite a rising population there were two million acres less under cultivation in 1938 than there had been in 1914: in 1934 wheat prices touched the lowest recorded point in nearly two centuries. Wages were far below the national average and farm workers abandoned the land to compete with the vast unemployed pool in the cities—testimony enough to the conditions in agriculture.

Aircraft factory: Spitfire assembly

Thousands of acres went derelict and the majority of cultivated land was given over to livestock, in particular to dairy farming. Prices for imported feeding stuffs were low: this made it just possible to make a profit in peacetime but created a dangerous unbalance in the first eighteen months of the war. The Cabinet, 'in a mood of muddled cheerfulness', believed that there were sufficient ships to maintain the import of feeding stuffs. Livestock farming actually rose, despite the fact that, acre for acre, land devoted to crops for direct human consumption produced a far higher food yield than that devoted to livestock. Then came the discovery that there were not, in fact, sufficient ships to allow the luxury of feeding animals and an emergency campaign was put in hand to plough up not only the derelict acres but also carefully nurtured grazing lands. The farmer was given a subsidy of two pounds for every acre ploughed up and the County War Agricultural Committees, known colloquially as War Ags, gave advice—and warnings. The War Ags had powers to dispossess farmers for incompetence and for refusing to obey a ploughing order and though these powers were used reluctantly and with moderation—members of the War Ag might very well be neighbours of the offending farmer—the net result was to transform a moribund industry into one of the foremost in the world. Mechanisation was introduced on an immense scale, beginning the end of the traditional methods even while it increased individual output by as much as fifteen per cent: by the end of the war the total number of working horses had dropped by a fifth, while tractors had increased from 60,000 to nearly a quarter of a million. Ploughing went on by night as well as day, the blackout regulations being waived for the purpose. By the middle of 1941 four million additional acres were under the plough and nearly two million more were added by the end of the war.

In some factories, as much as eighty per cent of the workforce was female, but farming remained a predominantly male occupation, women forming perhaps one third of the whole force. The Women's Land Army reinforced the traditional army of wives and daughters who had been brought up to regard farming as a way of life. The newcomers were almost all volunteers. It required a very positive motive, amounting almost to a vocation, for a woman to abandon the comforts of

Landgirls pause in their work to watch fighters returning

even a wartime city for the gruelling, lonely life of a farm-worker. Some of them formed mobile teams, directly employed by the local War Ag and despatched here and there, wherever their services were urgently required. These were perhaps the most fortunate, for they had the companionship of corporate life in hostels and their conditions of work and living were under immediate, official surveillance. Other women could find themselves on some remote farm, among people speaking a barely recognisable dialect, and treated as a species of slavey.

The WLA existed in a kind of official limbo. Its members were organised as a single group and were even issued with a uniform —a practical, not unattractive dress of khaki breeches, green jumper and wide-brimmed hat. A Land Army girl, uprooted from familiar surroundings, suffered all the homesickness and disorientation of her equivalent in the auxiliary forces and was as poorly paid. But she was denied the use of Forces can-teens during her brief leisure, had far less leave and more often than not had to pay her own fare home. Yet the wastage rate was lower than that in industry, the attraction of 'life on the land' surviving even experience of it. Some of them became specialists: cartoonists had much simple fun with the activities of lady rat-catchers. A number of girls volunteered for one of the loneliest jobs of the war, working for the Timber Corps. Those whose task it was to select trees for felling covered thousands of miles during the war, travelling alone or in tiny groups through the most remote parts of the country—and fre-quently being taken for spies in areas which rarely saw a stranger.

Townspeople responded to the call to 'Lend a hand on the land' during their summer holidays. Farmers welcomed them during harvest when a great deal of heavy, but simple work had to be performed in the shortest possible space of time. Their value was, at other periods, arguable, to say the least. Girls turned up dressed as for a picnic and were incapacitated in a matter of hours. The countryside which looked so idyllic from bus or train provided the smelliest, hardest work most townsfolk had encountered in their life. Some stuck it out, glad of the chance to earn a few shillings' pocket money in the fresh air but few repeated the experience. Servicemen from camps in rural areas were considerably more useful. Released from the tedium of barrack life, they gave a good day's work in return, for the bad worker was simply returned to barracks. From 1941 onwards there was the exotic addition of prisoners-of-war dressed in their blue dungarees with large green patches. Italians were far more popular than Germans. Most were actively glad to be out of the war and the guard over them was of the sketchiest. A working party of perhaps thirty or forty Italians, scattered over a wide area with a single soldier technically in charge, became a common sight.

During the Depression of the thirties thousands of unemployed men had turned to smallholding in a modest way as a means of whiling away the tedious days and filling the family larder. Local authorities rented allotments for a few shillings a year and a few more shillings-worth of seed could keep a family in vegetables for perhaps half the year. The 'Dig for Victory' campaign capitalised on the allotment movement in a big way.

The Ministry of Food propounded a simple but impressive equation: if the British love of gardening could be directed towards producing food instead of flowers and if the thousands of back gardens and allotments could be treated as the fragments of a titanic market garden, then up to a quarter of non-cereal supplies could be produced on a voluntary basis. The Ministry launched its campaign with a blizzard of leaflets, some couched in the usual exhortatory style, others giving solid advice and information. Cherished lawns disappeared from thousands of gardens, their place taken by rows of potatoes, cabbages, peas, beans. The King gave a lead. Windsor Great Park was put under the plough and, despite the headshaking of locals who predicted that the land would prove sour, it produced bumper harvests of wheat. Local councils followed: vegetables appeared in the trim flower beds of the parks, lawns were dug up, pergolas displayed crops of runner beans instead of roses.

Growing vegetables was merely an extension of gardening but thousands of people plunged enthusiastically into a wholly new activity—the rearing of livestock. Backyards which were too small or sunless, or whose vitiated soil could raise no crop, could yet give accommodation to half a dozen rabbits or chickens. For the first time in a century and more the drowsy clucking of hens sounded in the heart of the big industrial cities. By surrendering the household's egg ration it was possible to obtain a supply of poultry-feed to supplement the household scraps. Officially, those keeping more than twenty hens were allowed to keep only a proportion of the eggs produced, the remainder being surrendered to the local Food Office at the market price. The majority of town-dwellers contented themselves with less than twenty. The lucky or the skilful ones ensured themselves not only a supply of fresh eggs for the table but also a very useful item of barter; the unskilful ones could at least console themselves with roast chicken. Rabbits created a series of domestic crises when they were judged ready for the table. Hardier than hens and easier to feed they formed an excellent source of meat—but invariably acquired personalities during the fattening period and the decision to slaughter was never easy, particularly if there were children in the household.

The more ambitious joined pig clubs, run on a communal basis. Some members would be sleeping partners, contributing financially but leaving the rearing to the more expert. The clubs entered into direct competition with farmers for the contents of the swill buckets which now stood beside the domestic dustbin. They came under the searching gaze of the Ministry of Food: the Ministry was prepared to turn a blind eye to the elastic interpretation of the regulations concerning rabbits and hens—it would hardly have been possible to do otherwise, considering the numbers involved. But pig meat was so obviously an important source of food and the animals so very conspicuous that it was both vital and relatively easy to enforce the regulations. But the endless form-filling and the months of hard work received their triumphant justification in winter when the animals were slaughtered and each member of the pig club took home perhaps the equivalent of a month's ration of meat for the family.

A wartime shortage of food was to be expected in an island country which traditionally imported the bulk of its food supplies. The fact that that same island, built on coal, could also encounter a fuel crisis came as a painful surprise. How little it was expected was well attested by the fact that coal gas was used to supplement the petrol ration for cars in 1940 and that, in the same year, mining ceased to be a reserved occupa-

Firemens' pig club maintained on bombed site

Woman guard on underground—still newsworthy in September 1940

tion. Even when it became evident that a crisis was at hand, the War Cabinet moved slowly and reluctantly. The bitter memories of the Depression were still vividly alive and almost any action could be calculated to enrage either mine owners or workers. It was not until June 1942 that the Ministry of Fuel and Power came into being, supplanting the Mines Department of the Board of Trade, but still operating through the pit owners. Throughout the war the government uneasily rode two horses as far as the mines were concerned, baulking at the idea of nationalisation despite its overwhelming logic, yet claiming close control over development and running.

Ultimately, labour shortage was the cause of the crisis. It was no use appealing to the public to 'lend a hand in the mines': coal could not be mined on an amateur basis; it was impossible to tap that vast pool of female labour which now kept the factories going. Miners could be forced to stay in their jobs and the Essential Work Order was duly clamped upon them. Tardily, mining was recognised as a vital part of the war effort and miners were not only exempted from conscription but 33,000 miners who had already been called up were released from the Forces. Others, who had abandoned the moribund industry, were tracked down and directed to return to the pits.

But still the total fell short of what was required and at the end of 1943 Ernest Bevin took the extreme step of directing into the mines a proportion of the youths called up for National Service. The measure was universally hated. In theory, conscripts had been allowed to volunteer for the mines on call-up: in practice very few had done so. The young conscript, with reason, dreaded the prospect of life underground: even the Army appeared free and glamorous by contrast. But in December 1943 a literal process of decimation created an auxiliary force of miners—the Bevin Boys. The technique adopted was, perhaps, the ultimate in democratisation: one tenth of all registration numbers was chosen by ballot and the unfortunate owners of those numbers found themselves in the mines. Public-school boys, shop assistants, miners' sons—all endured the agonising uncertainty as their eighteenth birthday approached and, with it, the number that would set them apart from their fellows. Altogether, there were some 45,000 Bevin Boys, a small proportion of the 700,000 work force and of these less than 15,000 had the physical stamina to endure the gruelling work at the coal-face itself. In retrospect, the results hardly seem to justify the measure, but it had, perhaps, a valuable social result: 45,000 young men had first-hand knowledge of what conditions were really like in the industry that had made Britain's wealth.

Despite the Bevin Boys, despite the forcible return of reluctant miners to the pits, despite the Essential Work Orders, coal production actually fell. For the first time in his life the average miner realised that it was not necessary to half kill himself in order to earn a bare wage. As in other industries there was little incentive to earn large sums for there was little to spend the money on. The factory worker might decide to put in overtime in order to amass a nest egg; the miner preferred to turn his new-found cash value into leisure. Absenteeism rose; so did the letters to the press, recommending the execution yard for the loafing miner. The general public nursed perhaps an uneasy conscience about the whole business of the mines, but as absenteeism alternated with strikes so sympathy gave way not so much to anger as to a puzzled exasperation.

It was the private citizen who endured the full force of the effect of the unrest in the mines. Industry demanded and received generous supplies of coal: the domestic hearth and the local gas and electricity works went short. Parliament debated the possibility of introducing coal rationing: the principle of fair shares for all had, after all, worked well with all other vital supplies. But coal rationing was inextricably entangled with politics, both defenders and attackers seeing it as a means of advancing nationalisation. The newborn Ministry of Fuel and Power therefore fell back on the principle of 'voluntary rationing', and the public was subjected to yet another barrage of exhortations in a series of 'communiques' which sought to make the householder a soldier in the 'Battle for Fuel'. Some of the advice was sensible, even if it threw a curious light on the domestic arrangements of a people whose favourite topic was the vagaries of the weather. Lag your pipes, seal your windows, reduce the draughts from doors, the British were advised, 2,000 years after the Romans had first shown them how to keep their houses warm. But many of the communiques seem to have been produced simply to keep a journalist in occupation with their heavy retailing of the obvious, such as how to poke a fire, or their information that two people could warm themselves as well as one and therefore it was a good idea to share with the neighbours.

The British were made forcibly aware that electricity was a secondary, not a primary source of energy. Electric toasters, kettles, blankets now disappeared totally: the patriotic householder made do with a single low-powered electric light bulb where before there might have been a galaxy of lights. Small hotels and boarding houses welcomed the opportunity to save on the electric bill and their guests groped down stygian corridors in the name of patriotism. But it was the shortage of coal itself which caused the greatest distress, adding cold to the miseries of the blackout and exacerbating the effect of a low-energy diet. Domestic central heating was virtually non-existent and the supply of coal therefore heated only one room in the house. In most households, family life ebbed back to the kitchen in wintertime. In country districts the massive iron range was still the major means of cooking: designed to work on coal, it could be induced to consume wood but at so great a pace that the cooking of a meal became a major task. The countryman, however, could sit before the traditional log fire in his sittingroom. The city dweller had no such alternative. The evil smelling paraffin stove came back into its own, but paraffin was in as short supply as coal. Householders now took to gathering up the very coal dust: mixed with water and earth it could be

Rose-hips, collected by children,
were a valuable source of vitamins

made into a crude briquette which, if it did not put the fire out, would give out a little warmth. Baths became simply a means of removing dirt—and a chilly, uncomfortable way at that. The official recommendation was that the bath water should be only five inches deep and householders were urged to paint a line at that level. It became a nice point of etiquette as to whether to empty the bath after use, or leave it so that the next occupant could enjoy ten inches of lukewarm, dirty water instead of five inches of reasonably hot, clean water.

The voracious hunger of industry for raw materials caused an immense clearing out of attics and cellars and larders and the contents of countless forgotten cupboards. Next to the dustbin and the swill bucket, the good householder placed a neat pile of paper and cardboard, another of rags, another of bones— after they had been boiled and boiled again—and stacked bottles ready for the collectors. 'Salvage drives' achieved a popularity almost rivalling that of the War Weapons Weeks. Children played a large part in these, welcoming the opportunity to roam for miles, to poke about in other people's gardens and surreptitiously pocket some unconsidered trifle. The harvest was brought to local depots—and was frequently left there for months while the organic elements achieved an impressive degree of maturity, to the distress of neighbouring households.

Paper was one of the major 'targets'—a lot of it was needed to supply more leaflets to urge people to save salvage, including paper. At first the collectors' energy was fully occupied in moving the thousands of tons of old newspapers and magazines that were scattered throughout the country, but inevitably another and even larger source was located. A lady in Wiltshire drew attention to the rich harvest that could be reaped in Bloomsbury. 'As paper is so urgently needed, would it not be wise to make use of the thousands, or hundreds of thousands of copies of books stored in the British Museum? What better use could be made of them than making them serve their country?' The Trustees unpatriotically declined to serve their country in quite that fashion but other book lovers were not so delicate. In 1943 alone some fifty-six million volumes were contributed from private bookshelves around the country. Doubtless the majority of these deserved their fate: equally doubtless, many a rare book finished up in a pulping mill through ignorance or the fact that it was baled up with valueless material by accident. In most areas some sort of check was put into operation, the local libraries giving the consignments at least a cursory examination. About six million books were saved by this method, some being used to replenish the stock of bombed libraries, the rest being sent to the Inter-Allied Book Centre which was formed in 1944 to distribute books to the Forces. Ultimately the Book Drive was permanently to benefit public libraries, for the stock of the Inter-Allied Book Centre later formed the nucleus of the British National Book Centre which today distributes surplus copies between libraries.

Scrap metal was an obvious source for a vital material of war and objects which would have been ignored by any self-respecting totter before the war, now became the object of earnest interest in the Ministry of Works. The countryside showed a positive gain as old prams and bicycles and parts of nameless machines were tugged out of their long resting place in ditches and hedgerows. But the most obvious change was in the older parts of towns and cities where the British love of privacy had expressed itself in formidable barricades of iron railings. Plentiful, accessible and made of high-grade metal they became the subject of a compulsory order as early as May 1940 and for

Collection of iron railings

weeks afterwards workmen were busy cutting them down and removing them. Most people welcomed their departure— particularly those which fenced in the public squares and gardens. A *Daily Sketch* reader deplored 'the barbaric way in which they are being brought down by two-handed sledge hammers' and, as with the Book Drive, rare items undoubtedly found their way into the common pool. Here and there a determined owner successfully managed to oppose the order: the British Museum kept its vast barricade and so did the nearby gardens in Bedford Square. But in city after city the black, solid symbols of another age went into the crucibles of a new. Tradition and continuity were maintained in at least one London borough: a park-keeper in Hoxton regularly locked the gates at night, even though the railings had gone. 'I have never been told not to. It seems silly to me but I shall have to go on doing it until I am told not to.'

Further Reading
Keith A. H. Murray, *Agriculture** (1952). V. Sackville West, *The Women's Land Army* (1944). Ministry of Labour and National Service, *Report for the Years 1939–1946* (1947). W. H. B. Court, *Coal** (1951). Mass Observation, *People in Production* (1942). Inez Holden, *Night shift* (1941), mostly concerned with women in a small factory.

VII

The Strangers

Never before had there been such a mixing and a stirring of the population, such a confrontation of social mores. Typists from Kent found themselves manning lathes in Scottish factories; East End mothers stared unhappily at Somerset fields; shop assistants from Putney struggled with fire-hoses in Bermondsey; tough eighteen-year-olds from the back streets of Liverpool shared pithead baths with public schoolboys from Surrey. Norfolk villagers who looked on Suffolk villagers as effete foreigners found themselves playing host to black men from Louisiana. Throughout the country the monoglot British struggled to understand, or make themselves understood, to men from Poland, Denmark, Italy, France. Nicholas Bentley neatly summed up that aspect with his cartoon of the special policeman struggling to make head or tail of the polite request 'Prosza Pane, ktora jest najblizsza droga na Tottenham Court Road?' But the Geordie working on an East Anglian airfield, or the Welshman transported to Berkshire to make tanks found it almost as difficult to communicate with the natives.

Sixty million changes of addresses were recorded for the civil population alone, twelve million more than the entire population of the country. The same person might, forcibly, change his address on being bombed out; two or three more addresses could follow as he moved from temporary accommodation to temporary accommodation. Settled at last, he might be directed to a distant part of the country, necessitating yet another change in the much-thumbed personal identity card, yet another re-direction of personal mail.

The first wave of the internal movement took place two days

before the declaration of war. On Friday 1 September 1939 the mainline stations of all the great cities of the country were swamped with tens of thousands of young children and a smaller proportion of mothers; the scenes were repeated on the following two days until, by the evening of 3 September, nearly one and a half million women and children had been evacuated to safe areas. The 'evacuation' could have done on a major scale what a tiny handful of charitable societies had been struggling to do for years—to give the children of the slums the chance of a fuller, freer life in the open country. It left, instead, a scar on the national consciousness, the majority of hosts and guests alike looking back on the experience with a profound dislike. Two contrasting sides of Britain had been brought into enforced contact with each other and neither much liked what it saw.

Soldier, on leave, says goodbye to his child, proceeding on evacuation

The evacuation took place with a desperate sense of urgency: all other considerations were subordinate to the need to get the helpless away before the bombs began to fall. The fact that the bombs did not fall was no fault of the government and its reputation would indeed have been enhanced if the expected onslaught had taken place immediately and so dramatically justified the extreme measure. Viewed simply as a military operation, the transportation of nearly a million children in three days without a single child being killed, injured or even lost can be counted as a resounding success, the product of superb organisation. If the trains had been drawing away from burning cities then the absence of lavatories and cold drinks and the chaos in the reception areas would have been unimportant. As it was, the breakdown of the domestic side completely over-shadowed the operation as a whole.

The majority of the evacuees were unaccompanied children, over 800,000 in all. Early in the morning of each of the three days all evacuees were assembled at a number of pre-arranged points throughout the cities—in London, there were 1,600 of these points, the local school being an obvious first choice. At intervals throughout the day the children, all labelled with their names and addresses, were assembled in groups and marched off to the station or, in London, to the nearest underground station. The last that most parents saw of their children was as they marched away from the assembly point, departing 'for an indefinite period for an unknown destination, there to be committed to the care of strangers'.

The government had expected that at least three and a half million people would have taken advantage of the scheme: the fact that barely a third of the expected total arrived at the stations began the breakdown of the system. The timetable for train departures was drastically telescoped: as parties arrived so they were shepherded on to the first available train instead of waiting for the train that was scheduled for them. It was a sensible decision from the point of view of clearing the stations rapidly and continuously and, incidentally, reducing the tedious waiting period in the assembly points. But it was disastrous from the point of view of the reception areas. Welcoming committees waited for hours for trains that never arrived, or brought far more or far fewer evacuees than were expected.

Billeting officers who had prepared receptions for young children found that they had pregnant women on their hands; emergency dormitories in girls' schools remained empty while parties of adolescent boys had no beds for the night.

On the trains the excitement of departure gave way to tedium and acute physical discomfort. The authorities were forced to overlook the fact that small children tend to visit lavatories frequently. Those in charge of large parties were faced with an impossible problem on non-corridor trains: one such train, bound for Somerset from London, ended its journey in Berkshire when the cries of its passengers could no longer be ignored. The ordinary problems of wartime travel exacerbated the situation: journeys which normally occupied an hour or so took as much as four or five hours. There was no food to be had; washing was impossible; the children grew fractious, in turn irritating the adults. Already regretting their departure from home, bored, hungry, the evacuees were in a highly critical mood when at last they stepped out at some unknown station and confronted their hosts.

The standard of reception varied enormously from area to area. The government, so lavish with trains, so meticulous with preparations for departure, seemed indifferent as to what would

Evacuation of children: September 1939

happen at the other end: local authorities had received permission to spend money on reception preparations only three days before the mass exodus began. In some areas the fortunate arrivals were met by committees who had performed miracles of improvisation and who swept their charges from station to billets with the minimum of delay; in others, last-minute accommodation was found only by pressing appeals to charity or threats of compulsion. Desperately tired women, some in an advanced state of pregnancy, drearily trailed from house to house in the wake of the billeting officer; tiny children walked until they dropped asleep on to the pavement. Hindsight makes it easy to condemn the cold shake of the head and the slammed door yet, perhaps, it was a reaction to have been expected: as far as the householder was concerned a spontaneous decision made on the doorstep could result in acting as host to people of unknown habits and background for an unknown length of time. Thousands took that decision, opening the door and bringing in the homeless with no other motive than that of human compassion.

Even more humiliating to the sensitive were those scenes, described as resembling a 'Roman slave market' or a 'cattle auction' which took place in many reception centres when the local residents arrived to choose their 'guests'. Well-built boys were snapped up by farmers; grown girls who could 'help with the housework' found ready homes, as did attractive, neatly dressed younger children. But at every centre there remained a handful of dirty, unappealing children whom nobody wanted and who could be placed only through billeting officers exercising their powers of compulsion. The official billeting allowance of 10s per child—8s 6d if more than one child entered the same home—did little to ease the situation. It was just large enough to tempt the poorer householder to experiment in baby-farming while too small to cover more than bare essentials in any reasonably comfortable household.

The trains carrying the last of the evacuees in many cases passed the trains carrying the first of those returning, the first of those who decided, within a matter of hours, that bombs in the big cities were preferable to life in the country or in a small town. The disillusionment was, in part, the result of the big-city dweller's utter ignorance of country life and ways, in part, the result of a class confrontation. Tens of thousands of these mothers and children had never seen areas of green larger than the local park. The newspapers were full of 'human stories' about children who did not realise that milk came from a cow, that animals had to be killed to provide meat, that it was permissible to walk on the grass. The vast majority of children who did remain, adapted themselves swiftly and happily; the mothers found it impossible to do so. Accustomed to a warm hugger-mugger of life they found the open spaces disturbing, the closed inward world of the village claustrophobic, the lack of entertainments unbearable. On their part, scandalised villagers swopped stories of "'vacuee' mothers waiting for the Red Lion to open and of their children playing outside throughout the evening sustained by packets of crisps; of the free, ripe language with which mother and child communicated; of the mother's ignorance of elementary cooking.

In most rural areas, evacuees tended to be billeted with families in the same social stratum, the difficulties arising from conflicting ways of life rather than produced by differences of income. It was in the small towns with their rigid hierarchies, their social structures based on hair's-breadth differences of income that the result of the class confrontation was most pronounced. The majority of those who had been officially evacuated came from the ugly, industrial areas of the great cities. And those who lived in ugly, industrial areas did so largely because they were too poor to go anywhere else. In thousands of decent working-class and middle-class provincial homes, horrified citizens now had their first, direct contact with the result of grinding poverty. The sophisticated—or the saintly—could perhaps make the necessary distinction between the child and the habits imposed by that poverty: the ordinary householder, grimly trying to clean urine and excreta from a treasured carpet, only too often came to the unjust but excusable conclusion that the poor were dirty and nasty because they liked being dirty and nasty.

Meal times were a particular trial, quite apart from the irrational disgust aroused by alien eating habits. The housewife who had carefully prepared and served a balanced, wholesome meal had good grounds for irritation when it was pushed aside with demands that 'real food' such as fish and chips be

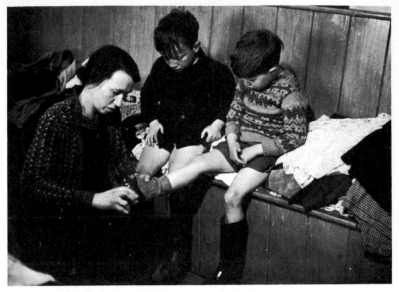

Clothing exchange for children

served instead. But the habits and equipment of a normal home were frequently incomprehensible to a slum child who had never had its own bed, never seen a fully equipped bathroom, possessed no other clothes than those for the street. A Dumfries housewife had prepared a bed with clean white sheets for the two children billeted on her. On the first night she went to see how they had settled down and found them pathetically huddled in a corner of the room: "We're no' goin' there," they said, pointing, "that's a bed for the deid folk."

Bedwetting, head lice and totally inadequate clothing were the three major problems. 'Somewhat unexpectedly, enuresis has proved to be one of the major menaces to the comfortable disposition of evacuated urban children,' the *Lancet* observed. 'Every morning every window is filled with bedding, hung out to air in the sunshine. The scene is cheerful but the house-holders are depressed.' In most cases the cause was obvious, the inevitable reaction of a small child on being torn up from its familiar little universe and dumped down among strangers in a strange land. But again the housewife, whose own children had long been housetrained, had cause to regret her generosity or the importunities of the billeting officer.

The trouble passed as the children settled down and, in any

144

case, the phenomenon could hardly be recognised as other than universal, likely to occur in the best run of families. Head lice, however, though occurring on a far smaller scale, produced a violent general reaction of disgust: comparatively few families had experienced it and the families in which verminous children were billeted could legitimately resent the possibility of the infection passing to their own children. Much of the trouble was due to the fact that evacuation had taken place at the very end of the long school holidays. Infestation which would have been detected by routine medical checks at school went unnoticed, and was then passed on during the crowded train journeys so that the incidence was increased beyond the norm. No official preparations had been made to inspect the children in the reception areas but as the horror stories multiplied, each improving in the telling, so local authorities took the law into their own hands. The medical officer in one of the reception areas for Liverpool courageously took the decision to crop the heads of all children coming into his area. The Liverpool area produced the highest degree of infestation with a startling maximum of fifty per cent. Elsewhere the proportion varied for no discernible cause: the London maximum was thirty-five per cent and Glasgow little more than a quarter. But after the first experience, every train load from every city was looked upon with suspicion and many a small child's heart was broken by the unfair taunt of 'lousy 'vacuee'.

In the first few weeks of the evacuation, it was usually possible to identify an evacuated child among a group of natives simply by clothing. Again, the contrast in the standards of clothing was as much a result of a differing way of life as of a differing level of income. The average farm labourer had, in fact, considerably less to spend on his children's clothes than the average industrial labourer. But the farm labourer's wife had been brought up in the tradition that it was more virtuous to mend than to throw away. The clothing clubs, with their deceptively easy method of obtaining frequent supplies of shoddy clothes, had not yet fully penetrated into the rural areas. Village boys still wore the solid, unglamorous boots of an earlier generation. Their capital outlay was greater, but they provided better long-term value than did the flimsy plimsolls or spuriously smart shoes of the city child.

Unemployment exacerbated the difference. It was the worker in London or Liverpool or Tyneside who was more likely to have experienced unemployment in the three years before the outbreak of war than the worker in Chipping Campden or Winchester or Bungay. Again, the long summer holiday had an adverse effect. Most parents equip their children for the autumn term towards the end of the holiday, the very poor inevitably postponing it until the very last days. The result was that hundreds of children were ushered to the trains dressed in clothing in the last stages of disintegration after a child's summer holiday. If the weather had been colder then even these would have been better dressed but that summer had been splendid, necessitating only the lightest and flimsiest of clothing.

Social habits, poverty, fine weather—these three factors combined to create a national problem. Rapidly, the alarmed reports began to pour in to the Ministry of Health. 'The town standard and requirements are much lower than that of the reception areas—especially in the small country towns. Many Manchester and Liverpool little girls have never worn knickers, a fact that distresses and horrifies the foster parents. A large percentage have never possessed sleeping suits, but take off the outer clothing and sleep in their underwear.'

The government reluctantly agreed to do something about the situation—but on a miniscule scale and with a cautious proviso: local authorities could spend up to £1 on boots and clothing for every 200 children but it was to be done discreetly, with no mention that the government was providing the money. The sum clothed the more dramatically ragged children but little else and it was upon the foster parents that the burden fell. It would have required an unusual degree of callousness, an unusual indifference to hygiene for foster parents to have tolerated the contrast between an ill-clad child and their own decently-dressed children in the same household. The stranger was dressed and the contrast eliminated, but it left another small residue of bitterness.

Unaccompanied children were either accepted or rejected: if accepted, perforce they became part of the household, subject to its discipline, fed and entertained along with the other children in the family. Children accompanied by their mothers

NOTICE.

MINISTRY OF FOOD.

MILK SUPPLIES

1. In order to supply any persons who, owing to the evacuation of their normal supplies, experience difficulty in obtaining Milk,

A MILK VAN

will be stationed in the following places every

MONDAY, WEDNESDAY, FRIDAY AND SATURDAY,

at approximately the times stated below :

APPROXIMATE TIME EVERY MONDAY, WEDNESDAY, FRIDAY and SATURDAY.

PLACE	TIME	PLACE	TIME
BLACKAWTON	9.0 to 9.15	CHILLINGTON	11.45 to 12.0
SEAWARDSTEIN	9.25 to 9.35	STOKENHAM	12.10 to 12.25
MILLCOMBE	9.50 to 10.0	TORCROSS	12.35 to 12.45
EAST ALLINGTON	10.15 to 10.30	SLAPTON	1.5 to 1.20
Hr. WALLATON CROSS	10.45 to 10.55	STRETE	1.45 to 2.0
SHERFORD	11.15 to 11.30		

2. THE MILK VAN can be stopped anywhere on its route. Residents in isolated houses are advised to arrange with others near or on the route to obtain their MILK for them. The route will be as follows :—Blackawton, Seawardstein, Millcombe, Pasture Cross, East Allington, Hr. Wallaton Cross, Coles Cross, Kingsbridgeford Cross, Stancombe Cross, Sherford, Oldcombe, Chillington, Stokenham, Torcross, Slapton, Homelands, Sea Cliff, Strete, Coombe Cross, Lower Wadstray.

3. The Van will bear a placard "Ministry of Food Milk Van." Except on Saturday, when the Bread Van does not tour the area, the Milk Van will be stationed at the same places and at the same times as the Bread Van on its route from Blackawton to Strete. Stopping times after leaving Strete will be :—Coombe Cross 2.5, Lower Wadstray 2.20 p.m.

4. Persons entitled to FREE OR CHEAP MILK under the National Milk Scheme, and those in possession of priority certificates, can obtain their authorised quantities either free of cost, or at the appropriate price, by signing the Milk Records-book, which will be carried on the Van.

5. BRING YOUR OWN MILK JUGS OR CONTAINERS.

MORTIMER BROS., PRINTERS AND PUBLISHERS, TOTNES.

What to do if the milkman is evacuated

147

existed in a kind of limbo, and for many of those mothers that limbo became a domestic hell. The cause of the friction between hostess and guest was nothing more dramatic, nothing more inhumane than the ancient problem of two women sharing the same, frequently limited, domestic offices. In certain cases relatives of the evacuated woman looked upon her billet as a free hotel and swarmed in to 'visit' her; in others, a resentful hostess deliberately made life as uncomfortable as possible to drive her unwanted guest away. But in the vast majority of cases an arrangement begun with mutual goodwill simply deteriorated under the stress of day-to-day living. It was fortunate that the good weather held, for the billeted woman could at least escape the tension by taking herself and her children out for the day. During September and October a common sight in small towns was the little knots of women and children drearily trailing from shop to shop, or queueing up for the afternoon cinema, simply to kill time until it was possible to go back to the single room in a strange house that was now home. The habit undoubtedly contributed to the widespread belief that all evacuated women were feckless creatures, preferring the pictures and the pub to domestic responsibilities. The tensions increased as the onset of winter enforced ever greater intimacy; simultaneously the need for it seemed to decrease as the threatened air-raids failed to occur. Throughout the country thousands of women thought longingly of their homes, reflected on the disintegration of their families, and came to a decision. Despite government exhortations to remain in the safety of the country, these women joined the returning flood so that by the end of the year more than three-quarters of all evacuated women and children had returned to the big cities.

Throughout the following years of war the numbers taking advantage of the official evacuation scheme rose and fell in two great waves, the peak of each coinciding with the major waves of aerial attack. Inevitably, it was the dark side of the scheme which coloured popular imagination. Among the tens of thousands of evacuees there were, inescapably, the amoral who exploited the position. On the other side there were, undoubtedly, an unpleasantly high proportion who dodged their communal responsibilities. A Ministry of Health survey of one town—which had declared its inability to take more evacuees—

found that there were, in fact, 8,000 spare rooms mainly in better-class residences and that the town councillors themselves had seventy-five spare rooms between them. There were many heartening examples of wealthy people throwing open their pleasant homes to children from the slums or near-slums but, as Richard Titmuss pointed out, in the main it was the poor who gave shelter to the poor. And the vast majority did it without compulsion. The powers were there but, though it was possible to place a child forcibly in a family, it was so obviously impossible to compel its acceptance, that the Ministry wisely left the decision to the discretion and powers of persuasion of the billeting officer.

The official evacuees formed only a part—and the smaller part—of the total number of evacuees. The government did not know it at the time, but while the Ministry of Health was puzzling itself as to why the numbers of evacuees were less than a third of what was expected, some two million people moved out of the cities on their own initiative. Many, perhaps the majority, simply took up residence with friends or relatives living in safe areas. The remainder were those who could buy safety. The desire to escape the consequences of total war was rational if not particularly noble. Most of those concerned could have contributed little to the 'war effort': the rigorous mobilisation of manpower regardless of class or sex made certain of that fact. But until conscription combed out the able-bodied, the 'funk-holes' of the rich acquired a great deal of notoriety in the press, a notoriety heightened by the hotel advertisements which frequently appeared alongside the article attacking them. Hotels in the remoter parts of the country discreetly made it known that their doors were open to the sensitive, to the artistic, to all those who wanted to shun the nastier aspects of a democratic war and who could pay for the privilege. Nathaniel Gubbins, the *Sunday Express* columnist, created the 'Safe Hotel' with its bored, selfish, well-to-do occupants, and the phrase passed into the language.

The fact that London, over the centuries, had acquired an immense social and commercial dominance led directly to another wave of evacuations. The administrative machinery of an empire was concentrated within a few hundred square yards around Parliament Square. Commercial organisations willingly paid vast sums for cramped, dark, totally inconvenient offices which were invested with the prestige of a central London postal address. A high proportion of the world's greatest hospitals were scattered among the nightclubs of Soho, the hotels of Bloomsbury, the warehouses and railway sidings of Southwark. Museums, art galleries, public schools, a university had grown up haphazardly and now lay side by side with legitimate military targets. It was impossible for all the institutions to move, the symbiosis proving indissoluble. But those who could put as much distance as possible between themselves and London.

The evacuation of the government's own departments created the most unpopular reaction of all. The organisers of the Civil Service exodus had the legitimate—the essential—task of ensuring that the evacuated department was kept together as a unit. Large hotels were the ideal billets. It was an inescapable equation whose results would have been accepted with goodwill had the operation been conducted with even a modicum of tact and good sense. The Office of Works, however, preferred to go about its work as though it were the arm of an occupying power in a conquered country. There had been time in plenty to warn certain hotel owners that, in the event of war, their premises would be requisitioned. Such warnings were not given, supposedly in the interests of security. What happened was that, within hours of the declaration of war, agents of the Office of Works began to call on hotel owners, ordering them to vacate their premises forthwith. The peremptory order would have been bad enough if applied to hotels with transitory populations. But such hotels usually occur in the centre of the larger cities and it was accommodation in the smaller towns and resorts that was naturally required. Hotel populations in this class of accommodation tend to be residential and owners frequently had the unpleasant task of telling aged residents, who might have lived in the hotel for thirty years or more, that they and all their belongings had to be out within twenty-four hours.

Officials commandeered what furniture they thought would be required, ordered the rest to be removed and sealed the hotel. Thereafter, many stood empty for weeks on end. Large hotel companies suffered heavy losses but the plight of the small owner-occupiers was pitiable. The hotel was not only their livelihood, the result of a lifetime's frugal work, but was also their home. Overnight they could find themselves in the street, saddled with debt and without an income. Altogether, nearly 300 hotels were commandeered, before the government, bowing to the storm that its methods had aroused, announced in November 1939 that no more were required. Under pressure, about 100 were returned to their owners and the incident passed into history. But it had given the British public a faint taste of what life under a totalitarian government could be like.

The centrifugal force of evacuation scattered institutions like autumn seeds across the country. A large part of the Admiralty found itself in Bath and apparently liked what it found, for it was still there long after the war had ended. Different sections of the Air Ministry rooted themselves in Worcester and Bristol: an intelligence division of the Foreign Office made itself at home in Woburn Abbey. Industry and commerce had to take second choice after the Civil Service had had its pick of stately homes and hotels. The white elephants of many an estate agent's list were hungrily snapped up: multi-million companies gladly refurbished mouldering Victorian villas, remote Georgian country houses and vicarages and even eyed medieval castles as possible asylums for their staffs. The members of these staffs joined in the scramble for local accommodation, competing with private and official evacuees and directed warworkers, and swamping the local services. But they brought with them, too, the habits of a larger world. Many a small town and village, whose entertainment in the past had perhaps consisted of an erratic cinema projector in a draughty hall, now found themselves playing host to sophisticated dramatic or arts clubs. Town councillors who had been content to jog along providing the barest minimum of social services were prodded by temporary citizens who expected more from their council than an occasional book van by way of a library, or an occasional brass band in the park by way of a concert. After the war, the majority of institutions and their staffs flooded back to London. But their influence remained and many a small community enjoys today social services which came into being as a result of the energy or importunity of their wartime guests.

By September 1939 some 60,000 Continental refugees, mainly

This Norwegian was ski-ing when the Royal Navy arrived at Lofoten. He left without removing his boots

of German and Austrian origin, had found asylum in Great Britain. Apart from the obligation to report to the police, the majority were free to pursue normal lives throughout the early months of the war, picking up a living in a strange land as best they could. Military intelligence was very much aware of the ease with which spies and Fifth Columnists could be introduced undetected in the mass of 'friendly aliens' but the leisurely atmosphere of the Phoney War made it possible to operate a reasonably fair sifting process. The police divided all aliens into three classes. A class was composed of the overtly hostile alien or disaffected citizen: the majority of these were interned within a few days of the outbreak of war. B class consisted of the borderline cases, including those who had only recently arrived in the country: their movements were restricted, they were subject to curfew regulations and were forbidden to possess map, wireless, car or bicycle. Class C contained the majority of aliens: German or Austrian nationals who had lived in Britain for at least six years, and political or racial refugees from the Continent generally.

The tension following the German breakthrough in the West in May 1940 abruptly altered the humane system of selection and tolerance. The Home Secretary at first moved slowly and reluctantly in response to the near-hysterical campaign in certain sections of the press to 'intern the lot'. But on 16 May all B-class aliens of German and Austrian origin were rounded up and over the following weeks the majority of even the inoffensive C class found themselves in internment camps.

It is probable that among the thousands of aliens swept into the bag there were one or two spies—or at least a handful of Nazi sympathisers. But it is debatable whether their seizure was justified at the cost of the widespread suffering it involved. Refugees from Nazi persecution endured again the terrifying experience of the knock on the door at night, the peremptory order to dress and pack a single suitcase, the departure by lorry or bus to an unknown destination. Families were split up, either because the members were in different classes or because they happened to be in different places at the moment of arrest. The English wife of an Austrian learned that her husband and son had been interned separately, the son being deported to Canada. Later, she was told that he could be released provided he returned straight home. 'Unfortunately this is out of the question as he was sent to Canada two weeks ago. We have no information as to his whereabouts. Who will pay his fare back? I cannot.'

The accident of geography could condemn a person to internment. A barrister who was paying for the education of a seventeen-year-old German Jewish boy at Winchester learned that the lad had been arrested because Winchester was in a 'prohibited area'. The barrister obtained permission for his ward to be educated in a non-prohibited area but meanwhile he had been moved from camp to camp and was then deported to Canada 'without even being allowed to pick up his belongings. If I had sent him to Rugby or Harrow or almost any other public school all would have been well. But how was I to know that I was doing wrong in sending him to Winchester?'

Officialdom frequently played a cat and mouse game, less

German nationals on the Isle of Man

out of sadism than from sheer muddle. Before her marriage to a C-class alien—a German of unimpeachable character—an English woman was told that she could reclaim her British nationality within two months of the marriage. Six months after the marriage her certificate had still not been issued, her protests being met with the remark that there was no need to worry as there was no time limit. Then her husband was interned and 'the official, with a characteristic gleam in his eye, observed that this of course changed the whole situation and that her status was now indubitably that of an enemy alien herself'.

The arrests were frequently brutal or, at best, tactless. Internment itself was not unpleasant. One of the internees, H. A. Schlossmann, described his experiences in the Central Promenade Camp on the Isle of Man. He found the authorities military but courteous and the conditions good, though over-crowding was a severe problem. Most of his fellow internees were philosophical about their experience, admitting the necessity and recognising the difficulties of administration. The most indignant protests came from those aliens who merely happened to be passing through England at the time and had been caught up in the general net. A very small minority of the internees were hardcore pro-Nazis.

Refugees continued to arrive in England at the rate of 800 a month until a total of some :50,000 was reached. A little more than a third of this total was composed of Jews but, in the popular mind, all refugees were Jews, giving rise to the insulting 'refujew' as a general term. Despite the fact that, by 1943, the British public were aware in fairly detailed terms of what was happening to the Jews on the other side of the Channel anti-

First day in England: Jewish refugee child, December 1938

semitism increased. During the London Blitz George Orwell conducted his own shelter survey to try and establish the truth, or otherwise, of the rumours that able-bodied Jews were taking shelter at the expense of women and children. He came to the conclusion that the story was just another vicious piece of nonsense. At the other extreme Douglas Reed thought it worthwhile to include in his book *All Our Tomorrows* a chapter, under the title of 'Enemy Natives', warning the country that it was in the process of being taken over by international Jewry.

The arousing of dormant anti-semitism was, in part, due to the simple insular dislike of the foreigner. 'The English Jew, wrote Orwell, 'who is often strictly orthodox but entirely anglicised in his habits, is less disliked than the European refugee who has probably not been near a synagogue for thirty years.' But, in the main, it was the traditional Jewish association with consumer industries—in particular with food and clothing—which caused most of the unpopularity. An irate customer, justly or unjustly denied some article in short supply by a Jewish shopkeeper, would add to the store of legend with accusations of a Jewish black market. Sometimes there was, in fact, substance to the accusations. The *Daily Mirror* columnist Cassandra, generally sympathetic to the Jews, noted: 'I have been examining the record of convictions for food misdemeanours and it is impossible not to be struck by the number of Jewish offenders. Names like Blum, Cohen, Gould and the like occur with remarkable frequency.' The charge was echoed by Janus in the *Spectator*. 'There can be no doubt that a section, and a substantial section, of the Jewish community has a black record in this respect. It is not to anyone's advantage to keep complete silence on the matter.' And in April 1943 the Chief Rabbi, Dr J. H. Hertz, took up the point in his Passover Letter. 'Though others are guilty of the same and of even graver transgressions, they do not in the eyes of the public compromise their religious communities. But every Jew holds the good name of his entire people in his hand.' The Jewish community set up tribunals to investigate rumours of Jewish black marketeering but even this could be used as an anti-semitic weapon on the argument that the tribunals were attempting to parallel the established courts and usurp their functions. Anti-semitism never became respectable: in the main its overt manifestation was limited to the poorer areas of the industrial cities. But it continued as a grumbling undertone until stunned into silence by the postwar photographs and reports of the concentration camps in Europe.

In the absence of any other news, it would have been possible to trace the progress of German arms on the Continent by the appearance of improbable foreign uniforms in the streets of British cities. First there had come the Czechs; then the Poles; then, in rapid succession, French, Dutch, Norwegians, Belgians. They jostled for accommodation with the troops from the Dominion and Colonial countries and, latterly, with the Americans until, by the eve of the invasion of Europe, nearly one and a half million soldiers from overseas were billeted in the country.

Polish National Day celebrated with solemn High Mass at Westminster Cathedral

Each national group had its clear-cut identity and its place in a kind of league table of popularity. The Czechs—square, solid, cheerful men—were universally liked. Opinion was sharply divided on the Poles. Their hosts, perhaps, half expected them to be grateful for going to war on their behalf and were inclined to be put out by the fierce, uncompromising nationalism which set them apart even among their fellow fighting exiles. Girls found them romantic; men regarded them, probably enviously, as showy. The Dutch and Norwegians were accepted with the casual ease of close relatives. Belgians were rather disliked, with the same general, unspecified dislike with which Jews were regarded. The French were known to be touchy and were treated with some caution, although they were popular enough. Of the Dominion troops Australians aroused the strongest feelings, being regarded with amused respect or profound dislike, depending on whether or not their host appreciated their larger-than-life qualities and their general air of having arrived in the nick of time to save the Old Country. New Zealanders were believed to be quieter and altogether more like the British; so, curiously, were Canadians despite their North American culture and accents.

There was probably a closer wartime affinity between the British and their Continental guests, despite the deep cultural differences, than between the British and their transatlantic cousins. The American authorities tacitly recognised the fact by publishing the admirable *Short Guide to Great Britain* for American soldiers in Britain. The book gave an excellent sketch of the British character as seen by a friendly, if slightly wary, observer. The GIS were warned that the British really did prefer to sit in silence in trains and buses and restaurants and were likely to take umbrage if their privacy was invaded, no matter how great the goodwill. The booklet's glossary showed how far the two languages had drifted apart from their common origin: biscuits and pies were no longer the same thing and great caution should be used when referring to suspenders and rubbers. Above all, the GI was warned to 'KEEP OUT OF ARGUMENTS. You can rub a Britisher the wrong way by telling him "we came over and won the last one". Each nation did its share. But Britain remembers that nearly a million of her best manhood died in the last war. America lost 60,000 in action. In the pubs

'Rainbow Corner': American social club in London

you will hear Britons openly criticising their government and the conduct of the war. That isn't an occasion for you to put in your two-cents' worth. It's their business, not yours.'

The American invasion struck the British Isles like a huge technicolor bomb, scattering nylons and cigarettes and candy and goodwill over the whole country. It probably affected every inhabitant of the islands from the farmer struggling to drive his tractor past gigantic vehicles in some narrow Norfolk lane, to the wondering young girl who saw now the incarnation of innumerable Hollywood films. The sheer prodigality of American equipment and supplies dazzled a population which had been cozened into accepting carrot flan as a kind of luxury. And the generosity with which those supplies were handed out was no less astounding. The Arabian Nights riches found their way into the eager hands of the British via hundreds of unofficial— and frequently illegal—routes: via civilian workers on the camps and airfields; via girl friends; via chance encounters in pubs; even via casual passersby. Towards the end of the war tobacconists became alarmed by the incredible quantity of fat, lovingly-packaged American cigarettes which were changing hands at a fraction of the price of the meagre English variety. The plump carton of Camels or Lucky Strike or Chesterfield was the favourite gift-offering of the soldier invited into a

British home. Small children learned that it was scarcely necessary to chant the ritual 'Any gum, chum' to activate the cornucopia of candy: all they had to do was to stand around in wistful-looking groups. The entertainments provided were on a similarly lavish scale. Dances at American bases brought glamour into the lives of thousands of young girls, confirming them in the belief that the centre of civilisation had long since moved westward.

One section of the population who remained disenchanted with the new allies was the British serviceman. The dislike was founded, understandably if unjustly, on the wide discrepancy in the rates of pay and standard of living. The basic American pay was nearly four times greater than the British—and few Americans, it seemed, drew the basic rate alone. The British serviceman's draughty canteens, dispensing curious tea and rock buns and reconstituted egg, contrasted ill with its American counterpart, comfortably furnished and dispensing coffee in prewar qualities, superb ice-cream, mouth-watering doughnuts—all, as often as not, free. The British were sadly handicapped in the serviceman's traditional recreation, the pursuit of women. It was by no means for purely mercenary reasons that girls were more attracted to these glamorous allies. The American dances, with their lavish buffets and first-class bands —some of them of international fame—belonged to another world than their British equivalent where rock buns again made their appearance and the bands were knocked together out of dubious local talent. The British gallant, too, held to an older, sturdier tradition of wooing where long grass played a more important role than a graceful handing out of taxis. Altogether,

U.S Soldiers and A.F.S girls

Children's party at U.S headquarters

it was understandable if his girl friend occasionally cast wistful glances at the renegade flashing by in nylons, on her way to dance to Glenn Miller and eat chicken Maryland. And it was undoubtedly a British serviceman who coined the immortal remark that the Americans were all right, except that they were overpaid, oversexed and over here.

Further Reading
The major source for the Evacuation and its ancillary problems is Titmuss *passim*. B. S. Johnson, *The Evacuees* (1968), contains the personal reminiscences of a group of evacuees looking back a quarter of a century later. For contemporary viewpoint see Richard Padley and Margaret Cole, *Evacuation Survey* (1940), and National Federation of Women's Institutes, *Town children through country eyes*. For aliens generally see Francois Lafitte, *The Internment of Aliens* (1940).

VIII

The Reflection of War

'Do you know Mr Secrecy Hush Hush, Mr Knowall, Miss Leaky Mouth, Miss Teacup Whisper, Mr Pride in Prophecy, Mr Glumpot? Tell these people to JOIN BRITAIN'S SILENT COLUMN, the great body of sensible men and women who have pledged themselves not to talk rumour and gossip and to stop others doing it.'

So, in July 1940 the British people, already dazed by a barrage of official slogans and exhortations, were urged to add six more symbolical figures to the national pantheon. The Ministry of Information spared no expense in its act of creation: whole page advertisements were taken in all the national dailies and magazines, photographic models engaged to create the parts. Mr Secrecy Hush-Hush: 'has always got exclusive information'; Mr Knowall 'knows what the Germans are going to do and when'; Miss Leaky Mouth 'simply can't stop talking'; Miss Teacup Whisper 'is a relative of Mr Secrecy Hush Hush'; Mr Pride in Prophecy 'is the marvellous fellow who knows how it is all going to turn out'; Mr Glumpot 'is the gloomy brother who is convinced that everything is going wrong'.

The characters, with names unhappily combining elements from children's comics and Puritan literature, covered a very wide range of potential sinners. Too wide—'a number of drunks and persons of feeble intellect have been clapped into gaol and given savage sentences for incautious explanations and a patriotic person has been arrested for saying "to hell with Hitler"—the explanation being that another patriotic ass had mistaken "hell" for "heil".' That was bad enough, but the underlying implication that a citizen's patriotic—and legal—

The Ministry of Information put out 2,500,000 posters in its anti-gossip campaign in early 1940

duty was to lay information regarding his neighbour's irritation with the war was far worse. The Silent Column campaign was received in a profound and ominous silence. Its verbosity compared badly with the laconic, precise, 'Careless Talk Costs Lives'; its condescending language irritated; its incitement to personal betrayals was alarming. For a week it was ignored, and then the storm broke. Dorothy L. Sayers noticed that the accepted media of communication took part in the attack only at the end, 'presumably because they carried the advertisements and freedom of the Press meant in practice freedom of control by anybody *except* the advertisers'. What she found particularly impressive was precisely the fact that there was no organisation of protest, no leadership. 'I only know that here was a thing that the people did not like and that mysteriously, with surprisingly little noise the great cumbersome machine of government went into action with the speed and force of an eighty-ton tank.' On 23 July, a little over three weeks after the campaign had been launched, Churchill pronounced its epitaph in the House, relegating it to 'innocuous desuetude'.

The Silent Column fiasco marked the low-water point of the Ministry of Information's public reputation. Since its inception it had been savaged steadily by Press and public alike. The Press resented its powers of censorship and feared its potential as a rival; the public mocked it as a ramshackle ivory tower giving shelter to a very curious collection of literary refugees from the hard facts of wartime life. Shortly after the outbreak of war Dylan Thomas tried to get an appointment, giving as his candid reason the fact that he wanted to avoid conscription

'because my one and only body I will not give'. His opinion of
the Ministry probably accurately summed up general opinion
at that time: 'I know that all the shysters of London are grovel-
ling about the Ministry of Information, all the half-poets, the
boiled newspapermen, submen from the island of crabs, dismissed advertisers, old mercuries, mass snoopers and all I have
managed to do is to have my name on the crook list.' The
extreme in criticism came with Evelyn Waugh's *Put Out More
Flags* with its hilarious, corrosive, grossly unfair but satisfying
portrait of the Ministry as a nest of lunatics, pansies and out-
right crooks. The Ministry, of its nature, was a ragbag of people
and objectives at the beginning of the war. Anything and everything could be classed as 'information', could be deemed able to
retard or accelerate the successful prosecution of the war
whether it were promoting viol concerts in the Midlands or
suppressing news about the sinking of the *Bismarck*. The left
hand only too frequently had no idea of what the right hand was
about. John Gunter, then a war correspondent in London,
asked for the text of one of the leaflets dropped over Germany.
His request was refused on the grounds that 'we are not allowed
to disclose information which might be of value to the enemy'.
Gunter then heavily pointed out that two million of these leaflets had just been distributed to the Germans. 'The man

*One of Fougassé's light-hearted, but
highly effective, anti-gossip posters*

".... strictly between
these four walls!"

CARELESS TALK
COSTS LIVES

blinked and said "Yes, there must be something wrong there".'
Harold Nicolson, at that time Parliamentary Secretary of the
Ministry, complained to the Naval representative that there
were no photographs of the sinking of the *Bismarck*. The reply
was an English classic. 'Well you see—you *must* see—well, upon
my word, well after all an Englishman would not like to take
snapshots of a fine vessel sinking.'

The unfairness of much of the attack on the Ministry was well
demonstrated by the campaign against its Wartime Social
Survey, a seemingly innocuous and, indeed, invaluable
organisation which was promptly dubbed 'Cooper's Snoopers',
after the Minister himself. Tom Harrisson and Charles Madge,
in their spirited introduction to Mass Observation's *War begins
at home*, had, in fact, argued for some such survey. 'Sociology
can, and should reflect and interpret public opinion instead of
the "public opinion" which is really the private opinion of
newspaper proprietors, BBC directors and the three or four men
who control the newsreels. . . . The Press, the BBC, the newsreels, Parliament, are living at different levels of income and
intelligence than the mass of people who left school at fourteen.'
Duff Cooper, the Minister, unwittingly echoed that judgement
when he attempted to defend the house-to-house canvassing
undertaken during the Survey. 'It is necessary to find out what
the people are really thinking, what is worrying them, whom
they trust and distrust.' But the spectre of the Gestapo over-
shadowed his earnest canvassers. The citizen saw, standing on
his doorstep, not an underpaid, temporary civil servant asking
harmless questions about his likes and dislikes but the anonymous arm of a threatening Government seeking to mould his
personal opinions. And if the citizen was slow to see that picture, the Press was swift to clarify it for him. 'There is only one
duty of the Ministry of Information,' the *Spectator* thundered,
'and that is to serve as a clearing house for distributing through
the proper channels—the Press and BBC primarily—all the
news which it can extract from the department and which can
safely be released.' Ironically, in the same issue of the *Spectator*,
its film critic deplored the lack of a research organisation to
check public reaction to the Ministry's own films: 'reports
from cinema managers, which are the immediate and easiest
way of checking, probably mean very little.'

Brendan Bracken, Minister of Information

Duff Cooper and his able, sensitive assistant Harold Nicolson, who together had borne the burden of the Ministry during its chaotic advent were removed, in July 1941, by what looks, in retrospect, more like an act of political butchery than surgery. The ebullient, red-haired Canadian Brendan Bracken, a personal friend of Winston Churchill's, took charge of the ill-formed monster and gave it a shape and purpose. That purpose was not to be the ideal conscience of the nation which had been envisaged at its foundation, but neither was it the truncated, emasculated thing that the Press demanded. Bracken skilfully steered his charge between the two extremes, the Ministry acting still as an instrument of censorship and news dispersal but also producing a considerable quantity of material in its own right—notably booklets on various aspects of the 'war effort'—convoys, firefighting, military campaigns and the like. It was, in effect, acting as a publisher and though many well-known names were commissioned to write the booklets, most remain curiously unreadable with an unpleasing echo of bombast and lack of hard facts. The Ministry was undoubtedly operating under the difficulty of being its own censor but it was an instructive demonstration of the fact that the State, for all its vast resources, did not necessarily make the best publisher.

The Ministry, as publisher, was in a remarkably favourable position in that it had access to generous stocks of paper. Official

165

publications as a whole were allotted 100,000 tons of paper per year: private publishing made do as best it could on a total allocation of some 20,000 tons annually, each firm's allocation being at first sixty per cent and then forty per cent of its prewar consumption. It was a rough and ready calculation but reasonably fair—except that it penalised the established publisher, who had to declare his prewar consumption and so obtain a reduced quota, in favour of newcomers who were allotted no official quota and could therefore use as much as they could pick up.

The respectable wartime publisher suffered agonies of frustration. On the one hand his paper stocks had been reduced far below his normal requirements; on the other was a public hungry for every type of reading matter. The danger and the discomforts of the blackout deterred all but the most dedicated pleasure-seekers from stirring abroad: long, dreary spells in air-raid shelters, or firewatching in deserted premises enhanced the value of books simply as boredom-breakers. The tens of thousands of servicemen and women alone formed a vast captive market as they endured those long spells of tedium which are as much a part of war as the excitement of danger. Reaching these print-hungry citizens was now a patriot's, not a salesman's duty: purchasers of magazines, and of the immensely popular Penguin paperbacks, were urged by the publishers to pass them on to the Forces when they had been read.

Book production, like some highly sensitive barometer, had reacted immediately to the pressure of war. In 1939, 14,913 new books had been published, a decrease of 1,178 on the previous year. In 1940 the number had sunk to 10,732; in 1941 it fell again to a little over 7,500. Enemy action now took an appalling toll of stocks: on the night of 29 December 1940, publishers' stocks totalling five million volumes perished in London alone; during the course of the war, four hundred libraries were destroyed. By 1941 more than 37,000 titles were unavailable: *Everyman's Library*, the poor man's university, could offer only 270 titles out of a total of 970.

Prices rose: most book-lovers were convinced that 7s 6d for a novel and 18s for a biography could be obtained only under wartime conditions and that the industry was pricing itself out of the market. The *Annual Register* took a different line. Price increases 'may have the effect of raising the standard of writing all round—a consummation devoutly to be wished', it noted in 1939—a pious hope which the flood of pulp material put out by ephemeral firms squashed firmly before the end of the war. As though the industry did not have sufficient domestic troubles the Government added its pin-prick which many saw as a potential death-thrust. In July 1940 Sir Kingsley Wood, looking round for luxuries on which to place his novel 'purchase tax', added books to the list. There was an immediate, hostile reaction in both Parliament and the country. 'Books are in fact weapons of war. Books project Britain abroad. How many citizens of the US are now with us because they have read Shakespeare or Dickens or Winston Churchill,' Lord Elton demanded. A. P. Herbert led the attack in the Commons, subjecting the Chancellor to a species of creeping barrage of questions, as witty as they were searching. The defenders of the tax brought to light that Puritan strain which manifested itself whenever there was a possibility to curtail individual liberty. The Member for Aylesbury argued that the public would benefit by being forced to go back to the already published classics instead of wasting its money on modern trash. The attack was beaten off and publishers were thereafterwards troubled only by lack of paper, lack of staff and aerial bombardment.

It was against this background of wholesale book slaughter and crippling financial limitations that the publishing industry struggled to maintain its traditional role of providing a medium for the reflection of society. There was a general expectation that the war poets and the war novelists would burst into song with the warbling of the first siren. But they obstinately kept silence: throughout 1939 and 1940 the literary weeklies were asking, with a hint of pettishness, what had become of them. George Orwell spoke for most when he noted in his diary that it was impossible to write under the prevailing conditions. Paradoxically, it was not until the war got into its stride, when the darkness was greater and the end out of sight, that the artists at last began to speak. But there were plenty to take their place. In 1940 the publishers' lists showed a heavy crop of books on religion and philosophy, responding to the hunger of a people who needed assurance and explanation for the cataclysm that had overwhelmed them. But it seemed that chatty works of uplift and solemn exegesis on the Christian religion did not provide the answer, for the proportion fell heavily in the following year and never again came anywhere near that first peak created by panic. Production of historical works declined. 'The incongruity of writing on past history amid the shattering events of the war was evident from the meagre output of historical studies,' the *Annual Register* noted. But publishers still found paper and patience and money to honour their traditional compact with scholarship: 1941 saw the publication of *Spanish Romanesque Architecture of the Eleventh Century*, 'the only complete history of the architecture of the Spanish eleventh century in one volume in any language', side by side with Erwin Panofsky's *The Codex Hugens and Leonardo da Vinci's Art Theory* 'an exhaustive analysis of a MSS in the Pierpoint Morgan Library'.

And there were the 'war books', the recounting of personal experiences, first coming in a trickle, then a gush and finally a flood which threatened to overwhelm every other form of literature. A few—a very few—were destined to survive as literature in their own right, unique sparks struck off by unprecedented pressures on the individual. Outstanding among these was Richard Hillary's *The Last Enemy*, celebrating the brief reign of the fighter pilot: Keith Douglas brought a more matter-of-fact approach to the soldier in his *Alamein to Zem-Zem*: John Strachey did the same for the air-raid warden in *Post D*. But the majority of these merely demonstrated that, while most people undoubtedly had a story in them, few could bring it out. Adventures of land girls and firemen, stories of soldiers on gun sites and in tanks, of sailors in submarines and destroyers, of airmen in aircraft, in their sum they presented an unrivalled picture of a society under abnormal circumstances, but individually are now as unreadable as the official publications. In a merciless passage in the *Spectator*, Simon Harcourt Smith summed up this vast class of book. 'The average warbook written by a serving combatant tends all too often towards the inarticulate or the two dimensional. How well we know them now—the modest warrior who claps all his adventures into two classes—"good show" and "bloody good show" or the type voluble in a strange language that has its roots in the road house era. "I pressed the tit and gave him a thirty-second burst.

Then the glass house bought one and so I had to do a brolly hop into the drink."'

Newspapers laboured under a dual disadvantage. Like books, they were subjected to drastic cuts in newsprint so that papers which, before the war, boasted of twenty pages and more were reduced to one double sheet. But, dealing as they did in the topical, they were also subjected to a rigorous censorship. Editors were unsurprised to learn that they would have to abandon weather forecasts: these could obviously aid the enemy bombers. The bombers, however, would apparently be aided if they knew what the weather had been like on the previous day: references to the weather had therefore to be several days old before they were permitted to appear. It was permissible to inform the British public that a given city in Germany had been raided on the night before, but it was not permitted to identify localities which had been bombed in Britain. The military censorship was, in the main, reasonable and was accepted without resentment but the bureaucrats' desire for secrecy only too often triumphed over the newspaperman's desire for information with unhappy results. Six months after Rudolph Hess had parachuted into Britain, in May 1941, the British public were still unaware of the reasons for his journey. Demands for information were parried with the practised statement that disclosure would not be in the public interest, even though well substantial rumours were circulating in America, and Stalin was publishing his own version in Russia. At the end of the year Commander King-Hall lamented: 'From the propaganda point of view, Hess was a great big unexploded bomb sitting in every German brain. But we defused him and made him into a dud. He is no longer news here or in Germany.'

The sweeping powers granted to the government made it as potentially perilous for a newspaper to criticise the conduct of the war as to disclose troop movements. The *Daily Worker* and the *Daily Mirror*, however, were the only papers to feel the edge of official anger. The *Worker*, dizzyingly trying to keep abreast of the party line, actively opposed the war during the period of the Russo-German alliance and was suppressed for its pains. The *Mirror* simply continued its habit of raucous disrespect for the mighty, its directors earning the distinction of being warned by the British War Cabinet and put on the wanted list by the

"The price of petrol has been increased by one penny"—Official

German High Command. It nearly suffered the *Worker*'s fate in March 1942 when the Cabinet took strong objection to Donald Zec's stark cartoon which showed a torpedoed seaman, adrift at sea, above the caption 'The price of petrol has been increased by one penny'.

In his book *Publish and be Damned* Hugh Cudlip described how the offending caption came quite casually into being. Zec showed the cartoon, with its original caption 'Petrol is dearer now' to his colleague Cassandra. 'You're a genius,' said Cassandra. 'But you want a stronger caption. You need to pin-point and dramatise the extra penny charge.' It is today difficult to read any other meaning into the cartoon but what Zec intended—that seamen were dying while civilians merely had to pay more and petrol therefore should not be wasted. Herbert Morrison, the Home Secretary, took the cartoon to mean 'that the seaman struggling on the raft at sea was risking his life in order that somebody might get additional profits. It was a wicked cartoon.' He summoned a director and the editor and threatened the paper with immediate suppression should such an incident occur again. Opinion in the *Mirror* office at the time was that the Cabinet had deliberately misinterpreted the cartoon in order to provide a weapon against a merciless critic but, looking back, Cudlip came to the charitable conclusion that 'Frayed nerves had led to distorted judgement'.

The cinema took an immense stride forward under pressure

of war. It still carried with it, however, the deadweight of the 'romantic' films which had been its staple before the war and was now adapted for wartime consumption. Predominant among these was the appalling *Mrs Miniver*, the sugary cinematic equivalent of *There'll Always Be An England*. 'Here is a film which trumpets a grandiose claim to present a picture of "ordinary" British people under fire, which begins with an elaborate peacetime essay in praise of social snobbery,' snarled one reviewer. Nevertheless, the film enjoyed immense popularity, the average British citizen apparently having no difficulty in identifying himself with the wealthy Minivers who owned a large car, an expensive motor boat, lived in a vast house by the river, possessed the services of a governess, two servants, boasted a son at Oxford and in general displayed 'fortitude in luxurious adversity'. The discerning could at least comfort themselves with the reflection that this was a Hollywood view of Britain. So too was the spurious *Commandos Strike at Dawn* with Paul Muni nobly sacrificing a military operation in order to rescue a prettily lisping heroine.

In September 1942 there appeared a genuine view of the war, Noel Coward's *In Which We Serve*, the first wartime film to treat working-class people as characters in their own right, and not simply as comic or loyal adjuncts to the romantic anguishes of their betters. The life of a destroyer at sea was faithfully portrayed even down to the use, on one occasion, of a single swear-word—a fact which earned great publicity for the film. *The Gentle Sex*, compered by the actor Leslie Howard, attempted a similar documentary realism for the ATS. Reviewing it, Edgar

Still from Mrs Miniver

Anstey praised it but remarked: 'The greatest fault is the basic assumption that women have never before undertaken hard, dangerous work. If Mr Howard is not torn limb from limb by working-class wives for this piece of middle-class myopia, he will scarcely survive the attentions of the factory girls in the next industrial town he may visit.'

The Crown Film Department of the much-abused Ministry of Information made an impressive contribution not only to British propaganda but also to the cause of helping the cinema to grow up. Its five-minute shorts took on average seven days to make and regularly appeared once a week. They were distributed both through the commercial circuits and through the Division's own mobile units which took them to factories, villages and small towns. Translated into fourteen languages, they later appeared in every major country of the world not occupied by the enemy. The subjects of most of them were simple, everyday events, telling the story of the British people's contribution to the war and how that war affected life in the country. *They Also Serve* portrayed the life of an ordinary housewife; *A Call to Arms* described how women adapted themselves to factory life; *Miss Grant Goes to the Door* was rather more fanciful with its tale of a Nazi parachutist ringing the bell of a country lady's home. *I was a fireman, Tobruk, Coastal Command* were workmanlike productions, free of ranting, their matter of fact style contrasting strongly with the strident, bombastic style with which the commercial newsreels treated similar topics. More ambitious, and wholly successful, was the overtly propaganda film *These Are the Men*, in which verse specially written by Dylan Thomas was superimposed upon Leni Riefenstahl's official Nazi film record of a pre-war Nuremberg Rally. 'When Hitler, Goering, Goebbels, Streicher and Hess speak we hear, instead of their original words, the ranting of homicidal maniacs confessing the crimes which had bathed the world in blood.'

The infant British television service died at noon on 1 September 1939 when some 20,000 domestic screens went blank without prior announcement. Sound broadcasting boomed, achieving a rapid maturity and a brief but total dominance over all news media, creating the single greatest difference between the First World War and the Second. The BBC's staff trebled in size, the number of licensed receivers soared by over a million until there was probably one for every four inhabitants of the country.

On the outbreak of war, all regional programmes closed down, their place being taken by a single Home Service programme. It embodied all that was earnest and uplifting in the pre-war BBC, epitomised by that *Thought for the Day* which Cassandra flayed: 'Threnody of each day's life! Death of each day's living! Five minutes of excruciating moralising before the morning news That Voice—so smooth, so soft, so suave.' News programmes came with the deadly regularity of hammer-

Demolition workers listen to
a broadcast speech by Winston Churchill

blows at every hour, interspersed with news flashes, official exhortations and cinema organ music. On 7 January 1940, however, the lighter Forces' Programme came into being and the BBC set out on its course of being all things to all men, an impossible goal which it came as near to achieving as any human institution is ever likely to reach. Sixteen million people listened to *Itma*—but probably every off-duty adult tuned in to the Nine O'clock News. In some ten million homes domestic life came to an abrupt halt as Big Ben boomed the hour, the family gathering round the bulky, clumsy receiver with its fussy fretwork as though it were some species of altar. The Big Ben Association specifically turned the occasion into a religious ceremony, its members uniting in silent prayer while the strokes of the great bell sounded. The news readers, who identified themselves by name to frustrate any Fifth Columnist takeover, became household names rivalling those of the established stars. Bruce Belfrage justly earned fame when he carried on reading the news with scarcely a break after a bomb exploded yards from him in Broadcasting House.

The five-minute *Kitchen Front* programme eased the burden of the housewife plotting rationed menus for the day. Scattered families were vicariously united through the request programmes—in particular *Forces' Favourites*, when each record was prefaced with a brief message from the serviceman choosing it. War-workers were made to feel a part of the national effort by the broadcasting of *Workers' Playtime* from the factories. *Music While You Work* spurred them on at the benches—and ominously heralded the Muzak of the post-war years. The BBC was prepared to experiment and its vast public, normal habits broken, was eager for novelty. A programme improbably compounded of a philosopher, a zoologist and a retired naval officer was tentatively put on the air on 1 January 1941. By the middle of February Cyril Joad, Julian Huxley and A. B. Campbell were known to millions and 'Brains Trust' had entered the language as a common term. Joad's shrill voice and favourite opening phrase 'It depends what you mean by . . .' became the property of every impersonator. The organisers of amateur entertainments would sooner or later fall back on the Brains Trust formula with its question-master and panel of impressed or self-styled experts. But the original never lost its freshness or popularity: towards the end of its life some twelve million people were listening to the Trust answering such questions as 'What is love?' and 'How do flies land on the ceiling?'

On Wednesday, 5 June 1940 those listeners who did not switch off when the Nine O'clock News ended heard a comfortable Yorkshire voice asking the question, 'I wonder how many of you feel as I do about this great battle and evacuation of Dunkirk?' The speaker was J. B. Priestley and he went on to reflect in a relaxed, deceptively casual way, on the significance of the armada of little ships which had taken part in the evacuation. The brief talk touched some chord of the national consciousness and, sensitive to that immediate response, the BBC shifted Priestley's *Postscript* to the peak period of the week—that following the Nine O'clock News on Sunday. Thereafter, the Postscripts were second only to the News itself in their ability to link the British together for a brief period of communal self-awareness. Their overt subjects were, in the main, trivial and ephemeral: ducks in a park; a drunk singing *Rule Britannia* in an air-raid; a clash with an official. Their delivery remained casual—the tone of voice one man might adopt when talking to another in a pub. But informing them was a deep, unselfconscious love of country, unmarred by bombast, which precisely reflected the temper of the people themselves during that summer and autumn. That temper changed. In his last Postscript Priestley himself remarked: 'The high, generous mood, so far as it affects our destinies here, is vanishing with the leaves. It is as if the poets had gone and the politicians were

J. B. Priestley taking part in BBC broadcast

175

coming back.' The politicians were indeed coming back: the speaker's outspoken views on a number of delicate subjects—in particular his attack on property—were deemed unsuitably controversial and after 20 October the Postscripts disappeared into history, though not without a great deal of unsuitable controversy. A little over a year later Graham Greene, reviewing the published edition of the talks, summed up J. B. Priestley's contribution to the air waves. 'There were many of us who, before the war made such disagreements seem trivial, regarded Mr Priestley with some venom. We felt that, as a novelist, he represented a false attitude to the crumbling, untidy, depressing world. Then, after the disaster of Dunkirk, he became a voice—a slow, roughened voice without the French polish of the usual BBC speaker. We shall never know how much this country owed to Mr Priestley last summer, but at a time when many writers showed unmistakeable signs of panic, Mr Priestley took the lead. When the war is over we may argue again about his merits as a novelist: for those dangerous months, when the Gestapo arrived in Paris, he was unmistakeably a great man.'

But the radio waves that could bring comfort and instructions and exhortations to the citizen before his own fireside could be used by the enemy to inculcate fear and disillusionment and German propagandists duly made use of the fact. On 25 February 1940 the New British Broadcasting Station went on the air, somewhat eccentrically using *Loch Lomond* as a signature tune and during the summer was joined by three other German-controlled stations—'Worker's Challenge', 'Caledonia' and the 'Christian Peace Movement'. The broadcasters purported to be British and the broadcasts themselves were a mixture of threats, boasts, and general appeals to the British to rise and throw off their tyrant leaders. In the critical months of 1940 they had a certain impact, for they seemed to substantiate the widespread fears that the country was riddled with Fifth Columnists and that German military might was overwhelming. But thereafter they dropped into the background.

Far more effective was the part sinister, part ludicrous figure of 'Lord Haw Haw' which British folklore was firmly to identify with William Joyce. Norman Baillie Stewart, who was broadcasting for the Germans while Joyce was still anxiously looking for work in Berlin, stated categorically that the first Haw Haw was Wolff Mitler, 'a man with both snobbish manners and an aristocratic voice: a playboy educated in Britain with an exaggerated "Oxford accent".' Stewart took Mitler's place and was then ousted by Joyce. There was, it seems a hierarchy even in hell and Stewart—a man who had succeeded in arousing the suspicion and hostility of the RASC, the Gestapo, the Seaforth Highlanders and the OKW at different times— was incensed by the way in which Joyce wormed his way into the broadcasts and finally emerged as the unique Lord Haw Haw.

Both Stewart and Joyce were plagued by the German 'experts' who frequently obliged them to use ludicrous scripts: a German airman 'made an emergency watering on the sea'; a battleship sank 'after being hit in the kettles'; the German flag had been 'hissed at Danzig'—an elementary confusion between the French *hisser* and the English *hoist*. Joyce was unable to persuade his masters that the term 'Lord Haw Haw' was not complimentary: the experts were convinced that every Englishman loved a lord. But all that was backstage. From the auditorium it seemed as though Lord Haw Haw were possessed of a frightening omniscience.

The broadcasts were listened to lightheartedly and even parodied commercially: the sneering introductory 'Jairmany calling' became a catchphrase to rival any of *Itma*'s. But Joyce retained sufficient control of his scripts to hit shrewdly at British hopes and fears, creating a series of fictitious characters who sometimes came uncomfortably close to reality—a Jewish millionaire, an incompetent diplomat, a hypocritical clergyman. But it was less what Haw Haw said than what he was believed to have said that made him effective. People created their own rumours, and then fathered him with them. In September 1939 Mitler had made the casual remark that the clock on a public library in a south Wales town was eight minutes slow. During the war that clock must have appeared in every British town. People told each other how Haw Haw had said that a factory was being built on the outskirts of the town, that an American had killed a British soldier during a drunken brawl, that the sugar ration was to be cut. Wisely, the government never made it an offence to listen to the broadcasts but it was perturbed enough by their effect to exhort the public to 'switch the blighter off' if they happened to pick him up on the wireless. And it was a testimony of William Joyce's success in probing the nerves of the British that this otherwise tolerant people killed him when they caught him.

Further Reading
The Annual Register passim for book production trends. John Lehman, *I am my brother* (1960), for wartime writing generally. Ronald Blythe, *The Components of the Scene*, an invaluable anthology of wartime prose and verse. Howard Thomas, *Britain's Brains Trust* (1944). J. B. Priestley, *Postscripts* (1940).

IX

Brave New World

Peace limped in as tardily, as unenthusiastically as the war itself had entered from the wings.

In the summer of 1944 there were confident predictions that it would 'all be over by autumn'. On the 11th September compulsory Home Guard parades ceased; on the 12th fire watching during the daytime came to an end. The blackout became a dimout: ice-cream returned—albeit in a curious, gritty form. On the war maps which garnished every newspaper the fat arrows writhed and stabbed from East and South and West, penetrating ever deeper into the German heartland. Yet, incredibly, the heart continued to beat. The news of the Ardennes offensive of 16 December did not bring despair, for the ultimate outcome was obvious and inevitable. But it ended any hope of bringing the conflict to a clear-cut end: the enemy was to be bludgeoned to death, the war was to drag messily and greyly on—long after every rational hope proclaimed its end. Abroad, the wartime unity of the Allies was already collapsing with British guns turned against Greek Communists; at home, there was already talk of a general election. Another fuel crisis coincided with a bitterly cold winter and early spring. Wearily, doggedly, the British trudged on to the end of the road. On 29 April the German forces in Italy surrendered; on 2 May Berlin itself fell; on 4 May German forces in North-West Germany surrendered. But still the hacked corpse continued to twitch as what remained of the German government in Flensburg attempted to negotiate a separate peace with the Western Allies. The British waited with an increasing sense of anticlimax but even after the war came to a final end at 2.41 a.m. on

The last V2: Farringdon Market, London, 10.58 a.m. March 8, 1945

7 May administrative muddle denied them a catharsis. Throughout that Monday crowds began to gather in the ceremonial centres of the kingdom: in London they flooded down the Mall and Whitehall, calling for the King outside Buckingham Palace, for Churchill outside Downing Street. No official announcement was made. The Government had agreed to announce the news in concert with its allies; they could come to no agreement and it was not until an American journalist at Eisenhower's headquarters had broken the embargo that the British public knew that the war had indeed come to an end. At 7.40 p.m. the BBC announced that the following day would be a public holiday: in order to stress the fact that only one war had ended, and that another was still in progress on the other side of the world, the day was to be known as Victory in Europe Day—a clumsy phrase rapidly abbreviated in the wartime manner to VE Day.

Over the next few months the distant war was to take on sudden reality for tens of thousands of servicemen. Warships of the Home Fleet began to exchange their dark blue Atlantic paint for the light blue of tropical waters: servicemen and women became acquainted with the comparative elegance of white drill and cotton. The Government began to sound a warning that all was not yet over: on a camp site in Leicester a conscript artist celebrated VE Day by putting the final strokes to a camp notice 'Don't lapse chaps: Japs!'. But the eastern war

was too far away, too remote in concept to act as more than a
general irritant to those not immediately affected and when, on
15 May, Bevin announced that three quarters of a million men
would be released from the services by the end of the year, the
thoughts of most turned to the immediate problems of peace, of
'building a new world', in the phrase of sloganeers of every
political colour. On 23 May Churchill formed a 'Caretaker
Government' in place of the dissolved wartime coalition. On
5 July the British went to the polls and, despite the immense
personal prestige of Winston Churchill, despite his warning
that a socialist government could not possibly operate without a
political police, elected 393 Labour MPs, giving a clear Labour
majority of 146 seats in the House.

There had been straws in plenty in the wind.

In autumn 1939 Weston Biscuits brought out the first of their
wartime advertisements. 'The duchess smiles a gracious smile.
Happiness has come to the ducal mansion,' the caption proclaimed as a liveried footman proffered her a box of the treasured biscuits on a silver tray. By 1942 the duchess had disappeared from the advertisements, her place being taken by
the sons and daughters of her tenants the 'lads and lassies' of
the armed services who now 'fairly took the biscuit'.

On the outbreak of war Harold Nicolson recorded: 'I hate
this war and dread its consequences. I know that whatever happens it will destroy everything I care for.' A year later he

Victory in Europe
May 8, 1945

happened to be listening to Priestley's last broadcast at the home of some aristocratic friends. 'There is, as always, that sense of mahogany and silver and peaches and portwine. All the virtues of aristocracy and none of the vulgarity of wealth. Priestley gives a broadcast about the abolition of privilege while I look at their albums of 1903 and the Delhi Durbar and the Viceroy's train. Priestley speaks of the new order which is to arise from the ashes. These two old people listen without flinching. I find their dignity and distinction and patriotism deeply moving.'

The less generous merely reflected that his hosts perhaps had excellent reason for patriotism, having enjoyed their silver and peaches and portwine undisturbed throughout the social chaos of the twenties and thirties. Many saw the war as a means of redressing the grotesque imbalance in society and even the moderate contemplated with equanimity the possibility of violent revolution to bring it about. Orwell thought that that revolution had actually begun in the autumn of 1940. 'Within two years, maybe a year, we shall see changes that will surprise the idiots who have no foresight. I daresay the London gutters will run with blood. All right, let them if necessary. But when the red militia are billeted in the Ritz I shall still feel that the England I was taught to love so long ago and for such different reasons is somehow persisting.'

The overt revolution did not occur, Orwell concluding, with something between a sigh and a shrug, that the British were just not adapted to take extreme action. But the revolution was nevertheless proceeding at a deeper, almost instinctive level. The bitter mockery of the 'Homes fit for heroes' slogan of the First World War was a personal memory for millions. On messdecks, in barracks, in desert camps the sons of those millions came back again and again to the question: what was going to happen 'when the lights went up'? The very fact that the War Cabinet declined to publish any formal war aims probably contributed to the slow, deep-moving current. The refusal was based on the reasonable assumption that a too narrow definition would disillusion, a too wide definition would prove impossible to honour. In the absence of such aims the people formulated their own. Almost every town and city in the kingdom prepared its 'post-war plans', visualising vague but splendid

Demobilised officers at clothing store

towers and avenues where now festered dreary brick. The current widened, drawing in schemes which, a decade earlier, would have been dismissed as impossibly utopian but which now seemed merely the blueprint of the essential. The Uthwatt Report of 1942 dared to suggest that it might be as well to impose some control on the use of land and out of it grew the Town and Country Planning Act of 1944 which erected the first great barrier against the spread of brick. The Education Act of 1944 created the Ministry of Education, imposed some form of order on the chaotic mosaic of local authorities and in general laid down the principle that education was not a reward for being rich but was a vital instrument of national well-being.

The great symbol of the new world that was going to be was the Beveridge Report of 1942. Hindsight has inevitably reduced the effect of its impact and even at the time there were many who were quick to point out that its provisions had long been accepted in principle. The novelty of the report lay not so much in its enunciation of the principle of assistance to all in adversity, as in the means whereby that assistance could be effected. If it had been published before the war it would probably have been dismissed as yet another academic exercise, discussed only by fellow academics. The upheavals created by wartime conditions made at least some part of its application essential, even while the questing new habit of mind seized upon its philosophy as something new and vital. Three weeks after its publication on 1 December 1942, a lengthy editorial in the *Spectator* noted

The return home

that 'the report has almost eclipsed the war itself as a subject of discussion'. A Gallup Poll had already disclosed that nineteen people out of twenty had at least heard of it—an astonishing proportion for an official publication—and nine people out of ten felt that its 'cradle to the grave' insurance coverage should be implemented. A correspondent in *The Times* belonged firmly to the one in ten. 'The way of the Beveridge report is the road to moral ruin in the nation: it is the way tending to weaken still further the spirit of initiative and adventure, the stimulus of competition, courage and self-reliance. It is a blow at the heart of the nation. It is the way of sleep.' The effect of the rolling periods was somewhat weakened when a correspondent unfairly pointed out that the writer was a prosperous stockbroker but others in high places tended to share his opinion. The Armed Services were to be protected against the report's moral enervation as far as it was in the power of the Minister for War: an edict went out banning discussions of the report at ABCA meetings. It had all the effect of an edict banning the advance of a tidal wave.

Further Reading
H. C. Dent, *The Education Act* (1944). Beveridge, William, *Full employment in a free society* (1944).

BIBLIOGRAPHY

General Works (specific works are listed at the end of each chapter)

Angus Calder, *The People's War*, 1969.

Sir Henry Channon, *The Diaries:* edited by Robert Rhodes James, 1967.

Winston Churchill, *The Second World War*, 1948–1954.

Basil Collier, *The Defence of the United Kingdom*, 1957.

Gallup Polls, *Public Opinion 1935–46*, 1951.

J. L. Hodson, (Diaries: published under the titles of) *Towards the morning*, 1941; *Before Daybreak*, 1941; *Home Front*, 1944.

Norman Longmate, *How We Lived Then*, 1971.

Harold Nicolson, *Diaries and Letters, 1939–1945*: edited by Nigel Nicolson, 1967.

George Orwell, *As I Please: London Letters to Partisan Review* in *The Collected Essays, Journalism and Letters*, 1968.

A. J. P. Taylor, *English History 1914–45*.

United Kingdom History of the War: Civil Series (Individual volumes identified by * in the lists at the end of individual chapters).

INDEX

unemployment, 1, 119
utility clothes, 86
utility furniture, 87

V1 (flying bomb), 73
V2 (rocket), 74
VE Day, 180

wages, rise of, 102
wardens and wardens posts,
  38–40
Wartime Social Survey, 164
welfare, *see* 'Bombed Out' Rest
  Centres
West Ham, bombing of, 53

Wilkinson, Ellen, 34
Women's Land Army (WLA),
  127
Women's Voluntary Services
  (WVS), 41
Wood, Kingsley, Secretary of
  State for Air, 24
Woolton, Lord, Minister of
  Food, 78–79
World War I, bombing casualties
  10: conscientious objectors, 44

xenophobia, lack of, 23

zone courts, 31